U.S. Immigration Policy

COUNCIL *on*
FOREIGN
RELATIONS

Independent Task Force Report No. 63

Jeb Bush and Thomas F. McLarty III,
Chairs
Edward Alden, *Project Director*

U.S. Immigration Policy

The Council on Foreign Relations (CFR) is an independent, nonpartisan membership organization, think tank, and publisher dedicated to being a resource for its members, government officials, business executives, journalists, educators and students, civic and religious leaders, and other interested citizens in order to help them better understand the world and the foreign policy choices facing the United States and other countries. Founded in 1921, CFR carries out its mission by maintaining a diverse membership, with special programs to promote interest and develop expertise in the next generation of foreign policy leaders; convening meetings at its headquarters in New York and in Washington, DC, and other cities where senior government officials, members of Congress, global leaders, and prominent thinkers come together with CFR members to discuss and debate major international issues; supporting a Studies Program that fosters independent research, enabling CFR scholars to produce articles, reports, and books and hold roundtables that analyze foreign policy issues and make concrete policy recommendations; publishing *Foreign Affairs*, the preeminent journal on international affairs and U.S. foreign policy; sponsoring Independent Task Forces that produce reports with both findings and policy prescriptions on the most important foreign policy topics; and providing up-to-date information and analysis about world events and American foreign policy on its website, www.cfr.org.

The Council on Foreign Relations takes no institutional position on policy issues and has no affiliation with the U.S. government. All statements of fact and expressions of opinion contained in its publications are the sole responsibility of the author or authors.

The Council on Foreign Relations sponsors Independent Task Forces to assess issues of current and critical importance to U.S. foreign policy and provide policymakers with concrete judgments and recommendations. Diverse in backgrounds and perspectives, Task Force members aim to reach a meaningful consensus on policy through private and nonpartisan deliberations. Once launched, Task Forces are independent of CFR and solely responsible for the content of their reports. Task Force members are asked to join a consensus signifying that they endorse "the general policy thrust and judgments reached by the group, though not necessarily every finding and recommendation." Each Task Force member also has the option of putting forward an additional or dissenting view. Members' affiliations are listed for identification purposes only and do not imply institutional endorsement. Task Force observers participate in discussions, but are not asked to join the consensus.

For further information about CFR or this Task Force, please write to the Council on Foreign Relations, Communications, 58 East 68th Street, New York, NY 10065, or call the Director of Communications at 212.434.9400. Visit CFR's website at www.cfr.org.

This report is printed on paper certified by SmartWood to the standards of the Forest Stewardship Council, which promotes environmentally responsible, socially beneficial, and economically viable management of the world's forests.

© **Mixed Sources**

Product group from well-managed forests, controlled sources and recycled wood or fiber
www.fsc.org Cert no. SW-COC-001530
© 1996 Forest Stewardship Council

FSC

Task Force Members

Task Force members are asked to join a consensus signifying that they endorse "the general policy thrust and judgments reached by the group, though not necessarily every finding and recommendation." They participate in the Task Force in their individual, not institutional, capacities.

Edward Alden

Mary Boies

Robert C. Bonner*

Jeb Bush

Allan E. Goodman

Gordon H. Hanson

Michael H. Jordan

Donald Kerwin

Richard D. Land

Elisa Massimino*

Thomas F. McLarty III

Eliseo Medina*

Steve Padilla

Robert D. Putnam

Andrew D. Selee

Margaret D. Stock

Frances Fragos Townsend

Kathleen Campbell Walker*

Raul H. Yzaguirre

*The individual has endorsed the report and submitted an additional or dissenting view.

Contents

Foreword

Few issues on the American political agenda are more complex or divisive than immigration. There is no shortage of problems with current policies and practices, from the difficulties and delays that confront many legal immigrants to the large number of illegal immigrants living in the country. Moreover, few issues touch as many areas of U.S. domestic life and foreign policy. Immigration is a matter of homeland security and international competitiveness—as well as a deeply human issue central to the lives of millions of individuals and families. It cuts to the heart of questions of citizenship and American identity and plays a large role in shaping both America's reality and its image in the world.

Immigration's emergence as a foreign policy issue coincides with the increasing reach of globalization. Not only must countries today compete to attract and retain talented people from around the world, but the view of the United States as a place of unparalleled openness and opportunity is also crucial to the maintenance of American leadership. There is a consensus that current policy is not serving the United States well on any of these fronts. Yet agreement on reform has proved elusive.

The goal of the Independent Task Force on U.S. Immigration Policy was to examine this complex issue and craft a nuanced strategy for reforming immigration policies and practices. The Task Force report argues that immigration is vital to the long-term prosperity and security of the United States. In the global competition to attract highly talented immigrants, the United States must ensure that it remains the destination of first choice. The report also finds that immigrants, who bring needed language and cultural skills, are an increasingly important asset for the U.S. armed forces. What is more, allowing people to come to this country to visit, study, or work is one of the surest means to build friendships with future generations of foreign leaders and to show America's best face to the world.

The Task Force finds that getting legal immigration right will also help policymakers tackle the issue of illegal immigration. As the terrorist attacks of September 11 demonstrated, porous borders can be a serious security vulnerability, and even as the United States welcomes immigrants, it must be able to control who is entering the country. The Task Force finds that the widespread presence of illegal immigrants has weakened the rule of law, created unfair competition for the American workforce, and strained the education and health budgets of many states. It also finds that taking steps to resolve the festering problem of illegal immigration is necessary for improving U.S. relations with Mexico.

The Task Force report recommends that Congress and the administration launch a new effort to pass comprehensive immigration reform legislation, built around a grand bargain with three elements: improvements to the legal immigration system so that it functions more efficiently to attract and retain talented and ambitious immigrants, a robust enforcement regime that secures America's borders and strongly discourages employers from hiring illegal workers, and a program of legalization that will allow many of those already living in the United States illegally to earn the right to remain. The report calls for new measures to bring in the best foreign students by removing many of the quotas and other roadblocks currently in place. It also recommends reconsideration of some of the post-9/11 border measures that have discouraged travel to the United States. Moreover, the report urges opening avenues for lower-skilled workers to come to the United States both temporarily and permanently, but with new mechanisms for adjusting the numbers based on the needs of the American economy. Finally, it calls for continued improvements in enforcement, including the creation of virtual borders to monitor entry, an electronic verification system for the workplace, and much tougher sanctions against employers who deliberately hire illegal immigrants.

On behalf of the Council on Foreign Relations, I thank Task Force chairs Jeb Bush and Mack McLarty, whose experience, wisdom, and passion for getting immigration policy right have underpinned this effort. CFR is also indebted to all Task Force members, a group of prominent individuals whose insights and expertise were indispensable. I am grateful to Anya Schmemann, director of CFR's Task Force program, who skillfully guided this project from start to finish. Finally, I thank

Edward Alden, CFR's Bernard L. Schwartz senior fellow, for ably and patiently directing the project and writing the report. All involved have produced a document that offers a clear and practical way forward as the Obama administration and Congress work to develop much needed changes to the U.S. immigration system.

Richard N. Haass
President
Council on Foreign Relations
July 2009

Acknowledgments

Some years ago, I had the pleasure of working as a newspaper editorial writer, a job that required meeting daily with a group of strong-willed, independent journalists and trying to hash out a common stance on the big issues of the day. Over the course of the many meetings, emails, and telephone conversations that led to this report, I have had many occasions to be thankful for that experience.

The report of the Independent Task Force on U.S. Immigration Policy is the product of a great deal of dedicated work and effort by the members of the Task Force, and I am immensely grateful for the time and care they devoted to this project. In particular, I thank our chairs, Jeb Bush and Mack McLarty, for their leadership and acumen in building consensus on what has too often been an extremely divisive issue. It has been a pleasure and a privilege to work with them and to learn from them.

The report benefited immensely from a series of outside meetings. Kay King and her team organized a preview event with CFR members in Washington, led by Task Force member Andrew D. Selee, and a session with ambassadors and other senior Washington diplomats who shared their views on how U.S. immigration policies have affected their countries. Task Force member Eliseo Medina arranged a meeting with representatives of church, labor union, and human rights groups to hear their perspectives. Nancy D. Bodurtha and her team organized a preview event for CFR members in New York, led by Task Force observer Shannon K. O'Neil. Irina A. Faskianos and her team organized a series of review sessions with CFR members across the country. I especially thank Task Force members Robert C. Bonner and Gordon H. Hanson for hosting meetings in Los Angeles and San Diego, respectively, and former Task Force member (now commerce secretary) Gary Locke for leading the meeting in Seattle.

Patricia Dorff and Lia C. Norton assisted in editing the report, and then readied it for publication. CFR's Communications, Corporate,

External Affairs, and Outreach teams worked to ensure that the report reaches the widest audience possible.

I am also thankful to the long list of people who met with me and various representatives of the Task Force, lending their advice and expertise to the topic, including Doris Meissner, who briefed us on the Migration Policy Institute's fine report. I note in particular the members of my CFR Roundtable on U.S. Border, Visa, and Immigration Policies, which has met regularly on these issues.

Anya Schmemann and Swetha Sridharan of the Task Force Program, and my research associate Andrew Rottas, were instrumental to this project from beginning to end, from the selection of Task Force members to the convening of meetings to the careful editing of multiple drafts. Andy also provided invaluable research assistance, unfailingly responding to my requests to delve into some other obscure region of immigration law.

I am also grateful to CFR President Richard N. Haass for giving me the opportunity to direct this important effort. We thank David M. Rubenstein for his support of the Task Force program and Bernard L. Schwartz for his generous support of CFR's work on American competitiveness.

Edward Alden
Project Director

Acronyms

AgJOBS	Agricultural Job Opportunities, Benefits, and Security
CAFTA	Central American Free Trade Agreement
CBP	Customs and Border Protection
DHS	Department of Homeland Security
DREAM	Development, Relief, and Education for Alien Minors
EU	European Union
GDP	gross domestic product
ICE	Immigration and Customs Enforcement
IRCA	Immigration Reform and Control Act
MPI	Migration Policy Institute
NAFTA	North American Free Trade Agreement
NEC	National Economic Council
NRC	National Research Council
NSEERS	National Security Entry-Exit Registration System
OECD	Organization for Economic Cooperation and Development
SBODAC	Secure Borders and Open Doors Advisory Committee
USCIS	U.S. Citizenship and Immigration Services
WHTI	Western Hemisphere Travel Initiative

Task Force Report

Introduction

The United States, a country shaped by generations of immigrants and their descendants, is badly mishandling its immigration policy, with serious consequences for its standing in the world. The urgency of this issue has led the Council on Foreign Relations to convene an Independent Task Force to deal with what is ordinarily regarded as a domestic policy matter. America's openness to and respect for immigrants has long been a foundation of its economic and military strength, and a vital tool in its diplomatic arsenal. With trade, technology, and travel continuing to shrink the world, the manner in which the United States handles immigration will be increasingly important to American foreign policy in the future. *The Task Force believes that the continued failure to devise and implement a sound and sustainable immigration policy threatens to weaken America's economy, to jeopardize its diplomacy, and to imperil its national security.*

Why is the country facing this crisis? Immigration should be seen as one of America's great success stories. The United States has for generations welcomed large numbers of immigrants, found productive employment for them, and successfully integrated them into its population. Unlike many other advanced countries, high levels of immigration have largely maintained what would otherwise be a shrinking population of working-age adults, a huge economic advantage for the United States. This country has been especially good at attracting ambitious, skilled people. For talented immigrants across the world, the United States has long been the destination of first choice. Many innovative and successful new American companies—Google, Intel, eBay, and countless others—have been built by recent immigrants. At the same time, the abundant opportunities for immigrants to advance and succeed here have largely spared the United States from the kinds of internal security threats that have faced European countries, where some immigrants are more marginalized.

America's attractiveness to immigrants is essential to its prosperity, and will be especially important in helping the United States recover and emerge stronger from the current global economic downturn. In a world in which many of the barriers to free trade have been eliminated, and high-wage countries are in direct competition with lower-wage countries, innovation is the essence of maintaining economic advantage. Innovation requires, more than anything else, an abundance of smart people with diverse knowledge and experience. No single country, however impressive its educational system, contains within its borders a preponderance of the world's most talented individuals. *The Task Force believes that one of the central reasons the United States achieved and has been able to retain its position of global leadership is that it is constantly replenishing its pool of talent, not just with the ablest and hardest working from inside its borders, but with the best from around the world. Maintaining American economic and political leadership depends on maintaining that flow of talent.*

Immigration has paid direct diplomatic benefits for the United States as well. America's openness to foreign students, investors, businesspeople, and visitors is a diplomatic asset that no other country has replicated. The State Department keeps on its website a list of current and former foreign leaders educated at American universities that runs into the hundreds. These U.S.-educated foreign leaders are enormously helpful for American foreign policy, providing a core of individuals in important positions across the world inclined to be sympathetic to the United States and its aims. Colin Powell, the former secretary of state, has said that foreign students "return home with an increased understanding and lasting affection for the United States. I can think of no more valuable asset to our country than the friendship of future world leaders who have been educated here." Robert Gates, the secretary of defense, has echoed that judgment: "In the last half century, allowing students from other countries to study here has been the most positive thing America has done to win friends from around the world." The current secretary of state, Hillary Clinton, said in a recent speech that "the benefits of such exchanges are so great that I am committed to streamline the visa process, particularly for science and technology students, so that even more qualified students will come to our campuses in the future." There is strong evidence that when students from nondemocratic countries are educated abroad in democratic countries like the United States, those who return home take those values with them and play an important role in trying to build democratic institutions in their own countries.[1] U.S. immigration policy has also been one of the more effective ways to encourage development in poorer countries. The United States has raised the living standards of millions of people around the world simply by allowing them to move here and earn higher wages. Remittances from the United States and other advanced countries to the developing world dwarf official development aid as a source of funds for many developing countries, amounting to more than $305 billion in 2008.[2] Many immigrants who succeed here end up returning home, bringing back needed skills and building economic links between their countries of birth and the United States, which help generate economic development that reduces the pressure to migrate.

Despite such extraordinary benefits, the continued inability of the United States to develop and enforce a workable system of immigration laws threatens to undermine these achievements. *The Task Force finds that the inadequacies of U.S. immigration policy have deprived the United States of some of the benefits that would otherwise be realized as a result of its generous immigration regime.* This is most apparent in the large population of immigrants living illegally in this country. Although the numbers have begun to fall in the current economic downturn, illegal immigration remains a serious problem. Nearly twelve million people are still living and working in the United States without the authorization to do so—a situation that diminishes respect for the law, creates potential security risks, weakens labor rights, strains U.S. relations with its Mexican neighbor, and unfairly burdens public education and social services in many states.

There are serious disagreements in this country over what should be done regarding the current population of illegal migrants, differences that have held hostage almost every other element of the immigration agenda. But there is no disagreement that the status quo is intolerable. The widespread presence of illegal immigrants offends fundamental notions of fairness, and calls into question what it means to be a sovereign nation. At the same time, U.S. efforts to crack down on the problem have at times led to harsh or arbitrary measures that are at odds with America's respect for the dignity and rights of individuals, most of whom are here in an otherwise laudable effort to better their lives and the lives of their families. The lure of higher wages or greater political and cultural freedom in the United States will continue to attract many to take the risks of migrating illegally. But, increasingly, they face a dangerous gauntlet of immigrant smugglers, stepped-up border enforcement, and the threat of criminal prosecution for the reward of what is often an insecure job that lacks basic workplace protections. Further, with the United States trying to tighten its legal visa and immigration regime to help prevent terrorist attacks by extremists coming into the United States from overseas, illegal migration also creates an unacceptable security risk, making it difficult for the government to know anything about millions of people who are crossing U.S. borders or already living in the country.

Although the United States has been unable to control illegal immigration, the legal system of entry is plagued by backlogs and delays, so that many people cannot come to this country in a timely fashion, or end up living here in a prolonged temporary status that provides little certainty for themselves or their families. This is the case both because of statutory restrictions on the number of people allowed to immigrate by country and category each year, and because of unnecessary delays in processing created by inefficiencies in the government and the large volume of immigration-related applications. These delays can drive some of the most talented individuals to other countries, and can force many families into long and painful separations. There is a widespread—and accurate—perception that the immigration system is not working nearly as well as it should be, either for Americans or for many of the immigrants. This country can, and must, do better.

The Task Force envisions an America that, recognizing both its rich traditions as an immigrant nation and the many benefits brought by immigration, generously welcomes immigrants through an orderly and efficient legal system. It envisions a nation that enforces sensible and understandable visa and immigration laws that welcome those who wish to visit, study, invest, and work here. It envisions an America that effectively controls and secures its borders, denying entry to those who are not permitted and denying jobs to those who are not authorized to work here.

As was apparent in the heated debates that accompanied the congressional effort to overhaul U.S. immigration laws in 2006 and 2007, such a vision will not easily be realized. There are many conflicting interests in immigration policy, and reconciling such differences is likely to be no easier in the future than it has been to date. But the stakes are too high to fail. If the United States continues to mishandle its immigration policy, it will damage one of the vital underpinnings of American prosperity and security, and could condemn the country to a long, slow decline in its status in the world. The Task Force is encouraged by the signals from the Obama administration and Congress that immigration reform will be a top priority.

Legislation is a critical part of improving the immigration system, and Congress has already laid some of the important groundwork. *The Task Force believes that the basic logic underlying the 2006 and 2007 efforts at comprehensive immigration reform bills remains sound—there needs to be a grand bargain that addresses three issues. First, there should be legislation that reforms the legal immigration system so that it operates more efficiently, responds more accurately to labor market needs, and enhances U.S. competitiveness. Second, the integrity of the system needs to be restored through an enforcement regime that strongly discourages employers and employees from operating outside that legal system. Finally, there must be a humane and orderly way to allow many of the roughly twelve million migrants currently living illegally in the United States to earn the right to remain here legally.*

Although legislation is important, no legislative reform will succeed without a commitment to improve significantly the current system for handling legal immigration and enforcing U.S. laws against illegal immigration. Much as the government has recently provided desperately needed resources for improving security at the country's borders and enforcing immigration laws more effectively, the United States must also invest in building and administering a modern, efficient system to handle legal immigration and temporary visa applications. No enforcement effort will succeed properly unless the legal channels for coming to the United States can be made to work better. *The Task Force believes that the U.S. government must invest in creating a working immigration system that alleviates long and counterproductive backlogs and delays, and ensures that whatever laws are enacted by Congress are enforced thoroughly and effectively.*

The report that follows is divided into three sections. First, it discusses how American national interests are at stake in its handling of immigration, and assesses how well current U.S. policies are serving those interests. Second, it lays out an argument for moving forward on comprehensive immigration reform in a way that opens doors to legal immigrants and closes them for those who try to skirt the rules. Last, it presents a set of recommendations both for changes to U.S. immigration laws, and for ongoing, incremental improvements in the functioning of immigration policies. While not intended as a comprehensive blueprint, the report lays out a series of principles and concrete recommendations that the Task Force believes must be at the heart of the U.S. effort to develop an immigration policy that better serves America's national interests.

*TABLE 1. A SELECTION OF WORLD LEADERS
WITH AMERICAN EDUCATION*

Country	Name	Title	University/College
Colombia	Álvaro Uribe Velez	President	Harvard University
Czech Republic	Václav Klaus	President	Cornell University
Georgia	Mikhail Saakashvili	President	Columbia University
Ghana	Kofi Annan	Secretary-General of the United Nations (former)	Macalester College, MIT
Greece	Kostas Karamanlis	Prime Minister	Tufts University
Indonesia	Susilo Bambang Yudhoyono	President	Webster University
Israel	Benjamin Netanyahu	Prime Minister	MIT
Israel	Shimon Peres	President	New York University, Harvard University
Japan	Taro Aso	Prime Minister	Stanford University
Jordan	Nader al-Dahabi	Prime Minister	Auburn University
Mexico	Felipe Calderón	President	Harvard University
Pakistan	Benazir Bhutto	Prime Minister (former)	Harvard University
Phillipines	Gloria Macapagal-Arroyo	President	Georgetown University
Republic of Korea	Ban Ki-moon	Secretary-General of the United Nations	Harvard University
Saudi Arabia	Bandar bin Sultan bin Abdulaziz	Secretary-General of the National Security Council	Johns Hopkins University
Taiwan	Ma Ying-jeou	President	New York University, Harvard University
United Kingdom	David Miliband	Secretary of State for Foreign and Commonwealth Affairs	MIT

Sources: U.S. Department of State; original research.

Immigration and U.S. National Interests

For any sovereign nation, deciding who will be allowed to live in the country is a fundamental question. The United States cannot permit everyone in the world who would like to live here to do so. Apart from the finite capacity of this country and its institutions to absorb such an influx, a completely laissez-faire approach of this sort would devalue what it means to be a citizen. Citizenship in any country comes with a series of rights and obligations, and it is up to America's democratic institutions to decide who should be invited to participate.

That premise, however reasonable and widely shared, is also the fundamental source of many of the problems that plague U.S. immigration policy. Immigration laws are designed to maintain limits to entry. They are intended to enforce quotas that restrict who can come here and to keep out those who are deemed undesirable—from the small number of terrorists and criminals who pose a genuine threat, to the much larger number who try to jump the queue in an otherwise laudable effort to improve their lives and the lives of their families. Like any rationing system, enforcing such limits is extremely difficult, particularly in the face of rapid population growth, ease of travel, and a more closely integrated global economy. Efforts at immigration reform must acknowledge the limits of any government's ability to control such large demographic and economic forces. U.S. immigration laws can be made much better, but, given the scale of the task, they will always be imperfect.

The United States, as a nation built and shaped by immigrants, has for much of its history had a more open door than most other advanced countries. Yet Americans, like people everywhere, have often been ambivalent about immigration. Although the tale of the impoverished immigrant made good is a fundamental part of U.S. history, the United States has been no more immune than any other nation to the fears that come when people who speak different languages, have different cultures, and embrace different faiths come to live together. And though immigration brings many benefits, a growing population places pressures on public services, and results in new competition for some jobs even as it creates many others and helps the economy to grow. Concerns over the costs of immigration inevitably rise either when the growth in the number of immigrants is large, or when the economy is experiencing a downturn. The United States currently faces both.

The United States has been absorbing close to one million new legal immigrants and until recently as many as five hundred thousand more illegal immigrants each year. In absolute terms, those are the largest immigrant flows in the world. Those numbers are shrinking in the current recession, which has dried up the job opportunities that are the magnet for many immigrants, especially for those not coming here to rejoin their families. Preliminary evidence suggests that illegal migration to the United States in particular has slowed dramatically over the past two years.[3] Less clear is whether the weakening economy and tougher enforcement measures are persuading illegal migrants already living in the United States to return home, though there is some anecdotal evidence that this is the case.[4] But even with a decline, immigration to the United States will still remain substantial compared to most countries in the world.

Immigration to the United States is large by any measure, but it is important to keep the figures in perspective. As a proportion of the population, the number of immigrants in the United States is close to that of other open, advanced countries: Australia, New Zealand, and Canada all in fact have higher percentages than the United States, and France and Germany are about the same.[5]

Immigration has long been considered primarily a domestic policy issue. During periods of high immigration, like today, the country has worried about its capacity to integrate new immigrants and to make them part of a cohesive American society. High levels of immigration also put pressure on many state and local services, particularly education and hospitals; state governments are forced to pay the costs for federal immigration policies over which they have no control. High levels of immigration also affect different parts of the country in different ways. Large, coastal cities have long been a magnet for immigrants and are accustomed to dealing with the challenges thrown up by immigration,

FIGURE 1. HISTORICAL LEGAL IMMIGRATION
TO THE UNITED STATES, 1820–2007

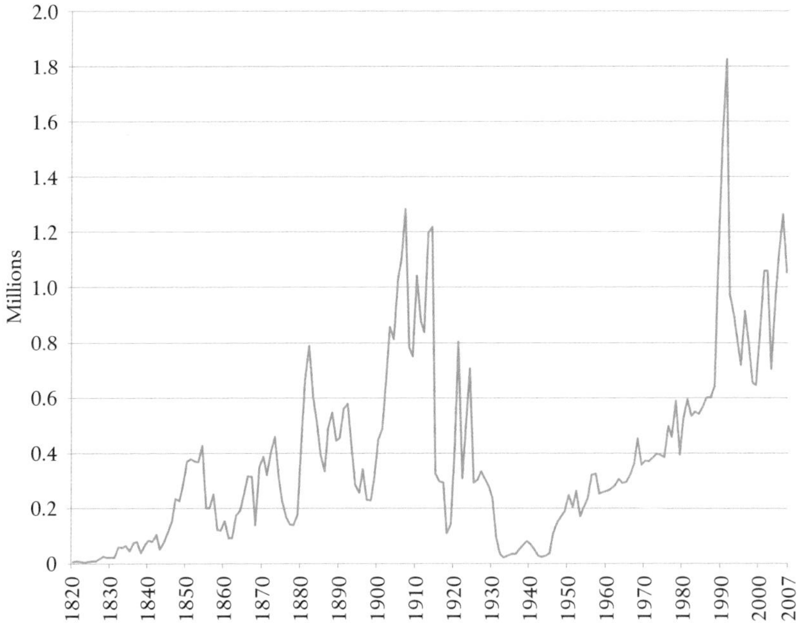

Source: Migration Policy Institute, 2008.

but the spread of immigrants into smaller cities and towns across the country has fostered new social tensions in these places.

Economically, the effects of immigration are also felt unequally. U.S. companies benefit from a larger, diverse workforce. Immigrants are concentrated at the lower- and higher-skill ends of the labor force, which tends to complement a U.S. labor force that is more concentrated in the middle. About 60 percent of native-born Americans have a high school diploma or some postsecondary education, whereas immigrants are clustered at the extremes, with many having either less than a high school education or a college degree or higher.[6] High levels of immigration put some downward pressure on wages, particularly those of lower-skilled Americans who have also seen their job opportunities and wages under pressure from liberalized global trading rules, though there is disagreement among economists on the

TABLE 2. TOP NATIONS BY NUMBER AND PERCENTAGE
OF IMMIGRANTS

Country	Number of Immigrants	Percentage of World's Immigrants	World Rank— Immigrants as Percentage of Population	Immigrants as Percentage of Population
United States	38,355,000	20.56	42	12.81
Russia	12,080,000	6.47	57	8.48
Germany	10,144,000	5.44	43	12.31
Ukraine	6,833,000	3.66	36	14.70
France	6,471,000	3.47	50	10.18
Saudi Arabia	6,361,000	3.41	19	25.25
Canada	6,106,000	3.27	25	18.76
India	5,700,000	3.06	167	.52
United Kingdom	5,408,000	2.90	55	8.98
Spain	4,790,000	2.57	46	10.79
Australia	4,097,000	2.20	23	19.93
People's Republic of China	3,852,000	2.06	187	.29

Source: UN World Population Policies 2005 report.

size of these effects.[7] Such domestic social and economic factors are obviously important in shaping U.S. immigration policies and influencing decisions about the mix of immigrants the United States wants to admit.

But there is another dimension that is equally important. Immigration has become increasingly central to American foreign policy, and crafting a more workable immigration policy is vital to U.S. foreign as well as domestic interests. The Task Force considers the six issues that follow—the economy, national security, America's image in the world, its core values, development policy, and the vital relationship with Mexico—to be the central foreign policy dimensions at stake in how the United States deals with immigration.

THE ECONOMY

Immigration has helped make the U.S. economy, despite its recent difficulties, into the world's strongest and most dynamic; maintaining that economic advantage is the foundation of America's influence and power in the world. If the United States loses its economic edge, its power will diminish. Getting immigration policy right is therefore critical to U.S. economic and political leadership.

More than half the recent growth in the U.S. labor force has come from immigration, and nearly all the future growth will come either from immigrants or from current workers delaying retirement.[8] Unlike Japan and most of Europe, which face a steady decline in their working-age populations, America's high immigration rates, and relatively high birth rates among more recent immigrants, have mitigated much of that decline.[9] Even countries seen as new economic rivals to the United States, such as China and Korea, face significant declines in their working-age populations and are becoming more interested in attracting immigrants themselves. *The Task Force finds that, though immigration will not substantially arrest the aging of the American population, openness to immigration means that the United States will face fewer of the economic and social pressures that will mount as a growing number of Americans retire and are supported by a smaller working-age population.* When the United Nations examined global demographic trends in 2000, it found that the United States was one of the few countries admitting enough migrants to expand its working-age population, though even the United States (and every other advanced country) is far short of admitting enough immigrants to maintain its ratio of working people to the retired elderly.[10]

The United States, along with other advanced countries, is producing many jobs in the service, retail, and leisure sectors that are not particularly attractive for native-born workers, but are a first step on the economic ladder for an unskilled immigrant. Immigrants are particularly overrepresented in sectors such as agriculture, construction, janitorial and maintenance work, and food preparation. The Bureau of Labor Statistics predicts that the majority of the fastest-growing jobs over the next decade will be ones that demand little or no higher education, including health, leisure, and hospitality services (though other low-skilled occupations such as stock clerks and cashiers will decline). Of the twenty occupations that will see the largest increase in the number of new jobs, twelve require only on-the-job training.[11] At the same time, the potential domestic pool of such workers has shrunk as a steadily higher percentage of native-born individuals have gone on to higher education.

There has been much debate over whether more Americans would be willing to do such jobs if they were more highly paid. The best answer is "perhaps," but there are many reasons why encouraging more Americans to do unskilled work would be difficult, would harm the economy, and would not be in the country's interests. Among the native born, fewer than 10 percent of the population fail to complete high school or its equivalent, and just over 60 percent are educated beyond the high school level.[12] Despite the growing number of low-skilled immigrants living in the United States, unskilled workers have continued to decline as a percentage of the overall labor force. Between 2000 and 2005, for example, the number of American-born working-age adults without a high school education fell by about one million.[13] Efforts to further restrict immigration by low-skilled workers and to lure more educated people into unskilled labor by raising wages for those jobs might be successful, but only at the cost of lowering the overall size and productivity of the economy by employing people at jobs below their skill levels. The net costs to the U.S. economy as a whole would be significant. There is a long history in the United States in which the influx of new immigrants has induced native-born residents to further their education, enhance their skills, and move up the occupational ladder; reversing this pattern would send the U.S. economy backward, not forward.[14] In some cases, businesses might adapt to immigration restrictions by making capital improvements rather than paying for a more expensive labor force, which would offset some of the productivity declines, but many of the fast-growing sectors for lower-skilled work are by their nature labor intensive, with limited prospects for capital substitutions.

Immigration's economic impact is not just a question of overall numbers. All countries, the United States included, try to attract skilled, educated immigrants who are likely to make the greatest contributions to the economy. In this effort, the United States has historically been extremely successful. *The Task Force finds that immigration has brought to the United States an inordinate share of the world's best talent, which has been a windfall in a global economy where heavy advantages accrue to the most innovative companies and the countries where they are based.* There is no question that the United States has enjoyed an enormous brain gain from immigration. In 2000, roughly 12.5 million legal immigrants in the United States had more than a high school education, and accounted for half of all the educated immigrants living in the Organization for Economic Cooperation and Development (OECD) countries. The second highest, Canada, had just over 10 percent.[15] More than one-quarter of U.S. immigrants have a bachelor's degree or higher. The United States has also done better than most European countries in attracting educated immigrants, though that advantage has been shrinking in recent years.

Other countries are recognizing the benefits that have accrued to the United States from being a magnet for foreign talent. The European Union (EU) is creating, though not without some controversy, a "blue card" that will provide easier entry into the EU for highly skilled workers and will allow them to work anywhere in Europe.[16] Canada has implemented a points system intended to identify immigrants whose skills are needed in the country and to make it easier for them to immigrate. Similar systems have been launched recently in Australia, New Zealand, and the United Kingdom, and are being considered in several other European countries.[17] In most cases, those systems do not include hard caps on the number of skilled immigrants who can be admitted each year. In contrast, the primary U.S. vehicle for attracting skilled immigrants, the H-1B visa program, is currently capped at 65,000 per year, with another 20,000 visas reserved for those who earned advanced degrees from American universities. In 2007 and 2008, despite some flexibility in the quota, it met less than half the demand for these workers from U.S. companies and was filled quickly after it opened each year. This year, with the severe recession sharply reducing job openings, the quota is likely to be large enough to meet most of the demand for skilled foreign workers.[18]

Some countries have also quite consciously tried to take advantage of American missteps, for instance, by aggressively recruiting foreign students who could not get visas to attend American universities after 9/11, or by offering permanent status to would-be immigrants to the United States caught in the lengthy backlogs for green cards.[19] Canada has increased the poststudy work period to three years and promised to facilitate permanent residence for foreign student graduates. Britain, which is second only to the United States in attracting foreign students, has invested aggressively to increase those numbers, aiming to add 100,000 foreign students between 2006 and 2011. The British government recently offered a new incentive by doubling to two years the time that foreign students can remain to work in the country after they graduate. As former prime minister Tony Blair put it, "It is about getting the skilled people we need into our economy, and building links around the world that could last a lifetime." However, the United Kingdom has also recently introduced far more stringent entry requirements for international students, leading to concerns in the higher-education sector that the new restrictions might negatively affect international student flows into the country.

There are new competitors as well. Japan, which has long resisted immigration, announced plans last summer to more than double its number of foreign students to 300,000 by 2020. It aims to simplify immigration procedures, to hire more English-speaking professors, and to assist students in finding jobs after they graduate. Some in the country are proposing a target of one million foreign students.[20] Singapore has set a goal of attracting 150,000 foreign students by 2015; Malaysia is aiming for 100,000.[21] Both Japan and Singapore subsidize tuition for foreign as well as for domestic students. India is making greater efforts to keep its advanced students at home. Even China is planning to offer scholarships for 20,000 foreign students and hopes to attract 500,000 by 2020. The United States is now facing a global competition for talent, and though it holds many advantages, it is no longer the only choice for the most talented immigrants seeking advancement.

The United States has tried in some ways to respond to this competition. The Department of Homeland Security (DHS), for instance, recently increased a postgraduation work program known as Optional Practical Training from twelve months to twenty-nine months for foreign students graduating with degrees in science, technology, engineering, or mathematics, a move that will increase the chances of foreign students in those fields finding permanent work in the United States. The State Department has made timely processing of student visas one of its top priorities, and the improvements have been significant. But U.S. laws and procedures, including the range of security and other background checks and the strict quotas on many categories of immigrant and nonimmigrant visas, still make it challenging for some foreign students and scholars to come to the United States to study and, if they wish, to remain here to work after they graduate.[22]

The Task Force believes that the costs of losing preeminence in attracting talented immigrants would be very high. The United States has hit a plateau in the numbers of American students graduating with advanced degrees, particularly in scientific and technical fields. Indeed, the number of science and engineering PhDs earned by U.S. citizens has fallen by more than 20 percent in the past decade.[23] The United States will face an accelerating shortage of highly skilled workers as the bulk of the baby boom generation starts heading into retirement. In 2006, there were more holders of master's, professional, and doctoral degrees among the age fifty-five to fifty-nine cohort, which is nearing retirement, than among the thirty to thirty-four cohort. More worrisome, this stagnation in the educational achievement levels of Americans has come at a time when many other countries—South Korea, Canada, Japan, France, Spain, and others—have continued to expand the share of their populations receiving higher education.[24]

In most developed countries that attract foreign students, higher education is an important path to permanent residence for highly skilled immigrants. Although the United States continues to host by far the largest proportion of globally mobile foreign students, its share has declined and other countries have gained ground. Enrollment, which had been growing rapidly in the 1990s, fell slightly for several years after 9/11. It began to recover in 2006 and 2007 to exceed pre-9/11 levels, rising to a record 624,000 international students in the 2007–2008 school year.[25] Overall, the number of foreign students attending American universities would have been about 25 percent higher if the pre-9/11 growth rates had continued.[26] Further, the sharpest drops were seen in first-time enrollment by foreign graduate students in science and engineering, which dropped by nearly 20 percent between 2001 and 2004 before beginning to recover in 2006 and 2007. They have yet to bounce back to pre-9/11 levels.[27]

Over that same period, foreign student enrollment surged in other countries: the United Kingdom gained 80,000 foreign students from 2003 to 2006, France and Australia each added 60,000, and Japan and Germany 20,000 each.[28] China, India, and some other countries have also done more to increase higher-education opportunities for their citizens at home. Overall, the number of students studying outside their home countries grew by 57 percent to nearly three million people from 1999 to 2007, the biggest increase ever. Yet the United States attracted only a small fraction of those new international students. Although it still hosts about 20 percent of the world's international students, roughly double its closest competitors (the United Kingdom, France, Australia, and Germany), other countries have been gaining ground.[29]

FIGURE 2. RECENT CHANGES IN INTERNATIONAL STUDENT
ENROLLMENT IN THE UNITED STATES, 1999–2008

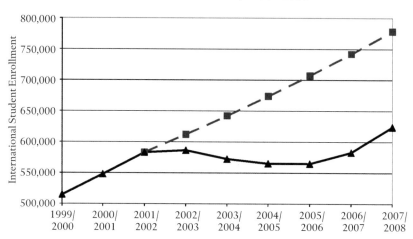

■— Projected enrollment (had growth rate remained unchanged; estimated average 4.94 percent)*

▲— Actual international student enrollment†

*Projected enrollment calculated by applying the average growth rate of 4.94 percent compounded annually from academic year 2001–2002 through academic year 2007–2008. The growth rate of 4.94 percent is based on the average rate of growth from academic year 1997–98 to academic year 2001–2002.

†This information represents international student enrollment data as reported by the Institute of International Education, *Open Doors 2008*.

Source: NAFSA: Association of International Educators, 2008.

The United States retains enormous advantages in attracting the world's best students. On any list of top universities in the world, American institutions predominate. Smaller countries like Australia have limited capacity to absorb new foreign students. In the United States, international students make up only 4 percent of total enrollment, suggesting that there is tremendous room for growth. But the competition has become much tougher than ever before.

The Task Force believes that immigration can never, nor should, make up for the deficits in the American educational system. It is critical that the United States reverse the trend that has seen fewer Americans pursuing higher education in the sciences and engineering. But education reform is a slow process that takes many years to show benefits, and even here many U.S. school districts are finding they must look abroad to find qualified teachers to fill positions in science, mathematics, and foreign languages. Immigration is necessary to fill those skills gaps.

Immigrants are especially important in science, technology, and engineering, which are so critical to U.S. economic competitiveness. Foreign students and immigrants make up more than half the scientific researchers in the United States; in 2006, they received 40 percent of science and engineering PhDs and 65 percent of computer science doctorates. Among postdoctoral students doing research at the highest levels, 60 percent are foreign born. This is not a recent development; even in the 1980s, some 40 percent of engineering and computer science students in the United States came from abroad.

On one significant measure of innovation, the number of patents issued each year, the United States far surpasses any country in the world; immigrants produce nearly 25 percent of those patents, or roughly twice their share of the U.S. population.[30] Other studies have shown that an increase in the number of foreign graduate students in the United States results in significant increases in the number of patent applications.[31] Overall, the share of all patents awarded to U.S. scientists of Chinese and Indian origin grew from just 4 percent in the late 1970s to 14 percent in the early part of this decade; at Intel, the world's largest semiconductor maker, 40 percent of the patents are for work done by Chinese or Indian immigrants. Just as important, this increased innovation by recent immigrants actually coincided with an increase in the number of patents awarded to native-born scientists as well, indicating that American-born and immigrant scientists are feeding off each other to enhance the country's overall innovative capacity.[32]

One in four engineering and technology companies established in the United States between 1995 and 2005 had an immigrant founder.[33] The four countries that create the greatest number of new companies per capita—the United States, Canada, Australia, and Israel—all have large immigrant populations.[34] It is not an overstatement to say that the United States would not enjoy anything close to its current technological and entrepreneurial leadership if it had maintained a closed immigration policy.

Amy Chua, the Yale historian and legal scholar, argues in her recent book, *Day of Empire: How Hyperpowers Rise to Global Dominance—and Why They Fall*, that the successful great powers in history have been those able to attract and make use of the most talented people the world has to offer. "At any given historical moment," she writes, "the most valuable human capital the world has to offer—whether in the form of intelligence, physical strength, skill, knowledge, creativity, networks, commercial innovation, or technological invention—is never to be found in any one locale or with any one ethnic or religious group. To pull away from its rivals on a global scale, a society must pull into itself and motivate the world's best and brightest, regardless of ethnicity, religion or background." America, she argues, has been more successful than any other country in the world in recent history in attracting and mobilizing such talents.

The Task Force believes that maintaining robust levels of immigration, allowing for fluctuations based on the state of the economy, is firmly in America's national interests. In particular, continuing to attract highly skilled immigrants is critical to the competitiveness of the U.S. economy, and to America's ability to remain the world's leader in innovation. The United States must open its doors more widely to such people.

NATIONAL SECURITY

Since the terrorist attacks of September 11, 2001, the United States has had to confront a difficult paradox: a generous immigration and visa system is potentially a threat to U.S. national security, yet is also critical to maintaining security. The nineteen hijackers who carried out the attacks were able to exploit weaknesses in the U.S. visa and border security regime to enter the United States and remain here unnoticed while they plotted and prepared for the attack. The ease with which they entered the country led to a series of measures aimed at making U.S. borders less vulnerable to infiltration by terrorists. Overall, as a result of such measures, the country is more secure from another terrorist attack than it was before 9/11. Yet some of those measures, by making it inordinately difficult for others to come to the United States, have the potential to weaken America's security rather than improve it.

Border and immigration policies can help keep terrorists or dangerous criminals out of the country. The United States can, for example, demand detailed background information, including fingerprints or other identifiers, from anyone who wishes to enter the country. Inspectors are free to search those arriving at the border, without any need to show reasonable suspicion or probable cause, as would be the case inside the country. On numerous occasions since 9/11, U.S. officials have also used minor immigration violations to deport people they believed were involved in terrorist-related activities, adding to the arsenal of law enforcement tools.[35]

The link between immigration policy and national security was institutionalized with the creation of the U.S. Department of Homeland Security in 2003.[36] DHS's primary mission is to protect the United States from another terrorist attack, yet the bulk of its personnel and resources are dedicated to the traditional tasks of immigration, trade facilitation, and border control. The post-9/11 debate about immigration has often been conducted in terms of a trade-off between security and openness, with advocates of tougher security willing to sacrifice openness, and proponents of openness prepared to run higher security risks. But that is only part of the dilemma. Indeed, the trade-off is also one between short-term security and longer-term security. *The Task Force finds that border and immigration measures, used in a targeted and focused way, can help make the United States less vulnerable to another terrorist attack. However, if those same measures keep out talented immigrants or significantly disrupt legitimate cross-border travel or commerce, the long-term foundations of America's economy and military strength, and consequently its security, will be weakened. The challenge is to find approaches that ensure that these two goals need not be mutually exclusive.*

The creation of the Department of Homeland Security accentuated an unfortunate tendency to define U.S. security in terms of who is kept out of the country rather than who is let in. The department regularly showcases statistics that highlight its success at barring people from entry: the number of criminal suspects or immigration violators turned away at the borders, illegal migrants apprehended or deported, and miles of fencing constructed. But those are incomplete measures of security. Although securing borders makes the United States safer from certain kinds of threats, especially terrorism and drug-related crime, the United States became a military superpower largely because of its economic strength and its technological capabilities, which have given its armed forces the most advanced and lethal weaponry in the world. Maintaining that status requires maintaining America's lead in innovation, and innovation thrives in an open environment. Gordon England, the former deputy defense secretary, put it strongly: "The greatest long-term threat to U.S. national security is not terrorists wielding a nuclear or biological weapon, but the erosion of America's place as a world leader in science and technology."[37]

As a recent National Research Council (NRC) committee report argued, many of the technologies that are vital for continued U.S. military superiority depend on scientific and engineering research occurring around the world, not just in the United States. U.S. national security and economic prosperity both require full engagement with scientific advances in other countries, and rely on attracting many of the best scientists and engineers to work in this country. "A leading American scientist in a cutting-edge field wants the very best scientific colleagues working with him or her regardless of nationality. An outstanding pool of talent working on a problem is the most likely path to significant scientific advancement," the NRC report says.[38] Rather than just measuring those kept out, the Department of Homeland Security, the State Department, and other agencies should also be keeping close track of the numbers of skilled foreigners being attracted to this country, and how the United States compares to other countries that are trying to draw from the same talent pool.

There would be serious negative national security consequences if the United States were to lose its technological edge. The technologies developed in the civilian economy of the United States are also vital for its military, and vice versa. Interaction with foreign companies and foreign scientists is inescapable and invaluable. U.S. technological leadership has by many measures already diminished; from 1997 to 2006, for instance, U.S. production of scientific articles in leading physics journals fell from 50 to 30 percent. Centers of scientific research excellence have sprung up around the world, and Japan, Korea, and several European countries have acquired leading positions in certain cutting-edge technologies.

America's national security depends on technological breakthroughs that keep U.S. military capabilities well ahead of those of rival nations. Yet a number of studies dating back a decade or more, which have looked not only at restrictions on the flow of scientists, but also at related restrictions on the export of technologies and scientific knowledge that might have military relevance, have found those efforts largely self-defeating.[39] There is a consensus in both the scientific and national security communities that measures aimed at limiting access to research and knowledge that could be used for harmful ends must be as narrow and targeted as possible to avoid hurting scientific enterprise. Yet that has not always been the practice.

In the aftermath of 9/11, for instance, the U.S. government expanded the so-called Visas Mantis program, which requires a special security clearance for students, researchers, and other temporary visitors to the United States who are knowledgeable in fields that could have national security implications. Consular security checks such as Visas Mantis resulted in long delays for students and scientists attempting to come to the United States, even for something as brief as a scientific conference.[40] Although improvements were made beginning in 2004, the effects have lingered. A recent new surge in visa delays associated with the background security checks has stranded hundreds of scientists and engineers already working at U.S. companies who had returned home briefly only to find they could not renew their visas in a timely fashion.[41]

Immigration can contribute to U.S. national security in other ways as well. The U.S. armed forces rely primarily, as they should, on U.S. citizens and permanent residents. But there is also a long and respected tradition in wartime of the military recruiting among more recent immigrants in an effort to bolster U.S. capabilities. *The Task Force believes that these immigrants are a valuable recruiting pool with language and cultural skills that are both enormously important for the conflicts of the twenty-first century and in short supply among Americans.* For example, the U.S. Special Operations Command—whose forces are on the sharp end of the global war on terrorism—sees cultural attunement, language proficiency, and local knowledge as critical operational skills no less important than the ability to navigate the terrain or fire a weapon. Yet, despite huge investments in language training, Special Operations remains seriously short on recruits with the language capabilities it needs. The more subtle aspects of cultural attunement and local knowledge are even more difficult to acquire. These are exactly the skills that those born abroad have, especially those native to the regions in which the conflicts of the future are most likely to take place.[42]

In an effort to expand its pool of suitable recruits, the military has sought authority to recruit immigrants living legally in the United States who do not yet hold green cards. In addition, Special Operations Command is interested in recruiting a few foreign nationals who have served courageously alongside U.S. forces in Iraq, Afghanistan, and other troubled spots. Under a 2002 executive order, those new recruits would be put on an expedited path to U.S. citizenship. Despite the critical military importance of recruiting such individuals, however, the White House has been reluctant to reopen the immigration debate by approving a large-scale program. Instead, it has authorized only a limited pilot program capped at one thousand new recruits a year, and restricted to those already in the United States who have medical training and certain specialized language skills.[43] *The Task Force believes that a more expansive program would pay substantial dividends.*

PUBLIC DIPLOMACY

America's image in the world has taken a beating in the past decade. The Pew Global Attitudes Project, the most comprehensive survey of its type, showed a precipitous drop in favorable opinions toward the United States from across the world between 1999 and 2008, with only a handful of exceptions.[44] The reasons for this decline are many, but the evidence is strong that immigration and cross-border exchanges of all types are among the best tools the U.S. government has for trying to reverse this decline. Certainly, mistreatment at the hands of U.S. border and immigration officials is one of the surest ways to denigrate America's standing in the eyes of many in the world.

Allowing people to come to the United States helps America's image by exposing foreigners directly or indirectly to the realities of life in this country. Polls of foreign attitudes toward the United States indicate strongly that those who have spent time here, or have friends or families who have spent time here, have more positive views of the United States than those who have not. In its polling of Arab countries, for instance, Zogby International found that Arabs who knew even a single American were roughly 10 percent more favorable in their opinion of the United States than those who did not. Among those who had traveled to the United States, wanted to travel here, or had a relative living here, the favorability was 25 to 30 percentage points higher. [45]

The Task Force finds that one of the most successful forms of public diplomacy has been to allow non-Americans to see what the United States has achieved at home. Encouraging travel to the United States has more positive influence than the best efforts that the government can muster to use the media and other channels to present a positive image abroad.

Yet, since 9/11, the United States has made it inordinately difficult for many people to travel here to see the country for themselves. This is especially true for those from Muslim and Arab countries where the need to improve understanding of the United States, and vice versa, is most urgent.[46] Visa restrictions put in place after the terrorist attacks, and special procedures such as the National Security Entry-Exit Registration System (NSEERS) that imposed extra screening on most male travelers from some two dozen Muslim countries, led to a significant drop in travel to the United States from all countries where visas are required. In the past few years, however, overseas travel recovered from most countries in the world to near pre-9/11 levels, but not from much of the Muslim and Arab world. In 2008, the number of visas issued to nationals of Egypt, Pakistan, Bangladesh, Jordan, Indonesia, and Saudi Arabia remained well below their pre-9/11 levels, in some cases half or less.[47] Although the United States must be vigilant in using its borders to keep out those who would do this country harm, there is significant scope for encouraging greater travel to this country without leaving it more vulnerable to acts of terrorism.

Apart from the aggregate numbers, the bad experiences that individuals may have while attempting to travel to the United States reverberate among their friends and families, damaging the perception of the United States as a country that welcomes foreigners. Steven Kull of the Program on International Policy Attitudes said that in focus groups with Arabs and Muslims "people very spontaneously brought up these restrictions on immigration and visas as evidence of . . . hostility toward Islam. Almost everybody in the focus groups knew somebody who had some problem when they came to visit the United States, or came to work here or to study here."[48]

According to a survey of two thousand international travelers from around the world commissioned by the U.S. travel industry in late 2006, the U.S. entry process was considered the world's worst by a two-to-one margin, with the Middle East a distant second. More than half the travelers said they found U.S. border officials rude and unpleasant.[49] Those officials represent the face of the U.S. government to much of the world, and it is critical that the face be a less hostile one. As former secretary of homeland security Tom Ridge put it, after 9/11, "the world was kind of surprised we pulled in the welcome mat so quickly." The Task Force believes the United States needs to put it out again.

Even before the current global economic downturn, overseas travel to the United States had yet to recover to pre-9/11 levels despite a surge in travel to other countries around the world. The economic costs, as well as the diplomatic costs, have been substantial.[50] A number of recent developments have been encouraging, however. The State Department and the Department of Homeland Security have worked hard to make the visa and entry process less onerous and more efficient. Both agencies have made progress in eliminating lengthy backlogs for security

FIGURE 3. INDICES OF NONIMMIGRANT VISAS
FROM NSEERS COUNTRIES, EUROPE, ASIA, AND THE WORLD

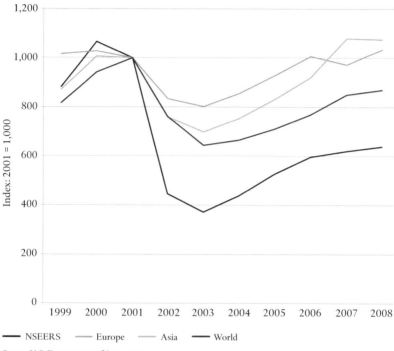

Source: U.S. Department of State, 2009.

checks that delayed many students and other visitors for months in
the aftermath of 9/11, although consular staffing shortages have occasionally caused the problems to recur. Over the past several years, for
example, waiting times for visas at most U.S. embassies abroad have
steadily declined; on the other hand, the delays for security reviews and
background checks that especially affect foreign scientists and engineers have unfortunately increased again, so that many visa holders
are facing waits of several months to return to the United States. U.S.
Customs and Border Protection has issued and prominently displays a
Pledge to Travelers and is training all frontline border officers to treat
returning travelers with courtesy, dignity, and a welcoming attitude.
Congress has also doubled funding over the past five years for educational exchanges such as the Fulbright program, which has historically

been one of the most successful U.S. public diplomacy initiatives. Although exchange programs of this sort are expensive, the payoffs are substantial in terms of building goodwill around the world and they should continue to be expanded.

In 2006, concerned about the slow recovery in overseas travel to the United States, the State Department and the Department of Homeland Security established the Secure Borders and Open Doors Advisory Committee (SBODAC) to make recommendations on how the United States could better attract and treat visitors without weakening efforts to protect the country's borders.[51] The report argued that the United States will become less secure if it implements measures that discourage people from coming to this country.

The Task Force endorses the core argument of the SBODAC report: "Our long-term success requires not only that we deter and detect determined adversaries, but also that we persuade millions of people around the globe of our ideals—democratic freedom, private enterprise, human rights, intellectual pursuit, and technological achievement. That persuasion requires human interaction, and each visitor to the United States represents such an opportunity." As the co-chairs of the committee wrote, "We cannot win the long struggle against extremist ideology by closing our doors to the people of the world [who] want to visit, learn and work here."

AMERICAN VALUES

America's immigration policy is an important part of its core values as a nation. The American dream remains a compelling ideal. Many people around the world believe fervently in the United States as a country where anyone, no matter how humble his or her origins, can start anew and succeed in building a better life. As pollster John Zogby has summarized the findings of his many international opinion surveys, "America still represents a beacon of hope."[52] Is it any wonder that the United States attracts not only many of the brightest, most capable migrants, but also many of the ambitious poor who see no opportunity for advancement in their own countries? For many in poorer countries, those who have braved the journey to reach the United States in an effort to better themselves and support their families at home are considered heroes. That many Americans see some of those same individuals as criminals is baffling to them. At the same time, however, many Americans worry that the failure to enforce immigration laws has betrayed an equally important part of the American value system—the commitment to the rule of law. They do not wish to reward those who are seen as having violated the law in order to come to the United States or remain here, and are skeptical of the government's commitment to enforcing immigration laws.

The Task Force believes that how the United States handles its immigration policy speaks to America's core values. Americans have a right to determine who will come to live in this country, and to enforce those rules, but they also have a responsibility to treat those who may have violated those rules with respect and fairness.

Enforcing U.S. immigration laws in their current state is an extraordinary challenge. An estimated twelve million people live in the United States illegally, but beyond their unauthorized status, they have little in common. Some were brought here as children and have lived in the United States for decades, retaining no significant ties to their birth countries; some have been here only a few months. Some have no family ties; many have U.S. citizen relatives, including spouses and children.[53] The vast majority are hardworking and, apart from their undocumented status, law abiding, but some are serious criminals tied to transnational gangs and other criminal organizations. Many have no plausible legal claim for remaining in the United States, but many others do. Somewhere between one million and one and a half million persons of the total illegal immigrant population in the United States are estimated to have a claim to legal status, but are stuck waiting for their cases to be considered because of the backlogs or administrative processing delays.[54] Yet the systems for enforcing immigration laws do little to allow for distinctions among these very different cases.

To take one example, the United States has greatly expanded the number of noncitizens who are detained for extended periods. In the 2007 fiscal year, nearly 311,000 such people were jailed, triple the number of a decade ago.[55] The policy has been driven by the necessary goal of trying to ensure that those who are ordered removed do not simply disappear and remain in the United States unlawfully, which has been a long-standing problem, or that those seeking asylum do not pose a security threat. As recently as 2005, some 60 percent of those arrested for violating immigration laws, and then subsequently released and ordered to appear in court, failed to show for their removal hearings;

fewer than one in five of those ordered deported actually left the United States.[56] Since the end of these so-called catch-and-release policies in 2006, virtually all non-Mexican unauthorized immigrants are now detained, compared with just 30 percent as recently as 2005.[57]

Ensuring that deportation orders are carried out is an important goal, and was largely ignored for too long. Yet the expansion of detention has resulted in individuals sometimes being jailed for months, even years, as their legal cases grind through overloaded immigration courts. Long detentions have caused some would-be migrants and asylum seekers to give up their claims for legal status. Medical care and other treatment for those detained have often been woefully inadequate.[58] And detention has been expanded, though there is growing evidence that less restrictive measures, such as supervised release programs, can still ensure that the vast majority of those facing deportation comply with the law, and at much lower costs.[59] The DHS inspector general has urged the department to move ahead with cost-effective alternatives to detention, in part to ensure that it has enough facilities to detain those who pose a genuine risk if released.[60]

Since the mid-1990s, Congress has tried to establish a reasonable set of priorities for enforcement efforts, particularly by directing that the highest priority for deportation should be those convicted of a serious criminal offense. Criminals, and those deemed to pose a national security threat, must be jailed until they are removed, and the law allows for almost no exceptions. But as enforcement efforts have grown, they have reached well beyond those convicted of serious crimes. Congress in 1996, for instance, expanded the category of aggravated felons, who even if they are green-card holders or other legal residents face automatic deportation for their crimes with no right of appeal. Most drug crimes also result automatically in deportation. The policy makes sense in general; the Task Force believes that immigrants who commit serious crimes should forfeit their right to remain in the United States. The problems arise when deportations are carried out without any consideration of specific circumstances. In some cases, the crimes are not what one would ordinarily think of as aggravated offenses—such as shoplifting or fraud. These deportations take place without any weight being given to an individual's circumstances, such as family ties in the United States, the time that has elapsed since his or her conviction, and the severity of the crime. In addition, individuals can be deported for offenses that sometimes took place many years ago. Legal immigrants held under the aggravated felony provisions are automatically jailed until they are deported, and once deported are permanently barred from returning to the United States. There are no good data on the number of individuals deported under the aggravated felony provisions; the best estimate is just over 150,000 cases over the past decade.[61] *The Task Force believes that serious criminals—those who commit felony offenses—can and should be deported, even if they are in the country legally. The United States needs, however, a more discriminating system that separates serious offenses from minor ones, and allows for greater flexibility in dealing with extenuating circumstances.*

Further, the complexity of U.S. immigration rules is such that harsh treatment can be inadvertently visited upon innocent individuals. The workplace raids carried out by Immigration and Customs Enforcement (ICE) officials, though a legitimate component of immigration enforcement, have sometimes resulted in U.S. citizens being mistakenly detained and even removed from the United States. Recent investigations by the *Associated Press* and the *Los Angeles Times* uncovered dozens of such cases.[62] And some of those clogging up immigration court proceedings are people who have tried to comply with U.S. immigration rules but have fallen through one of the many cracks that make it easy to inadvertently forfeit legal immigration status. These include individuals whose cases have been in limbo because of excessive visa application processing delays.

Other measures enacted with the reasonable goal of ensuring tough enforcement of immigration laws have nevertheless made U.S. treatment of some immigration violators, as well as some legal immigrants, unnecessarily inflexible. Congress in 1996, for example, passed a law that prevents immigration violators from returning to the United States for up to ten years, and sometimes permanently, even for what are occasionally minor or technical immigration law violations. These penalties can make it impossible for individuals who might otherwise be entitled to remain in the United States to find any legal way to do so. Some U.S. citizens now find that their parents, spouses, and children are barred from the United States for a decade, or even permanently, as a result of these laws.

The treatment of refugees and asylum seekers is another dimension of immigration policy that reflects important American values. U.S. refugee policy has been among the areas of immigration policy most closely tied to foreign policy priorities. Throughout the Cold War, for instance, the United States had an open door for those fleeing Communist countries or other U.S. adversaries, but cast a far more skeptical eye on those facing persecution in countries allied with the United States. While refugee policy has historically been used to serve other foreign policy interests, it has largely been driven by the ethical conviction that those fleeing political, religious, or other forms of persecution should be offered safe haven. That commitment is enshrined in international treaties and domestic U.S. laws that set the standard for the rest of the world; when American standards erode, refugees face greater risks everywhere. U.S. refugee and asylum policies have also opened this country to an array of impressive scientists and others fleeing persecution in their home countries, a tradition that continues with contemporary efforts to rescue scholars facing oppression abroad.[63]

Historically, asylum claims had been particularly susceptible to fraud, in part because for those without family ties or employment skills, such claims represent one of the only remaining legal channels for migrating to the United States. For many years, those who arrived in the United States and claimed asylum were routinely allowed into the country and issued a permit that would allow them to obtain a Social Security card and to work pending a hearing on their claims. Substantial backlogs meant it would be many years before an invalid asylum claim would be detected.[64] Not surprisingly, a significant number failed to show at their hearings and simply remained in the country illegally.[65] Moreover, well before 9/11, there were fears that asylum claims could be abused by terrorists attempting to enter the United States, as they had been in the past. Ramzi Yousef, the chief architect of the 1993 bombing of the World Trade Center towers by Islamic radicals, entered the United States on a false Iraqi passport, claimed political asylum, and was released into the country pending a hearing. The asylum system was reformed in the mid-1990s in order to better protect against fraudulent claims. The long delays that had allowed individuals to stay in the United States for years while awaiting an asylum interview were eliminated. Instead, those who request asylum quickly find themselves in deportation proceedings if their request is not granted by an asylum officer after an interview, a procedure known as expedited removal. In addition, those who request asylum are no longer given automatic work authorization, eliminating an incentive that had encouraged some to file baseless asylum claims. Congress also passed broad legislation that made it more difficult for genuine refugees to access the U.S. asylum system, and mandated initial detention for those who arrive in the United States without valid travel documents.

After 9/11, in an effort to keep out those who might have ties to terrorist groups, Congress and the administration established extremely broad definitions of "material support" for terrorist groups that had the unintended effect of barring individuals who in the past would certainly have gained admission. Some prodemocracy opponents of authoritarian regimes in places like Burma, Cuba, and Iraq, for example, were excluded on material support grounds; in one well-publicized case, an Iraqi who was teaching Arabic to U.S. Marines was labeled as a supporter of terrorism because he had worked to overthrow Saddam Hussein. In other cases, the material support provisions had the effect of barring asylum seekers who were forced to assist terrorist organizations under the threat of death or severe injury. After much delay, the Bush administration made some progress by issuing waivers in the most egregious cases, but serious problems remain.[66]

Partly as a consequence of the new restrictions, there was a sharp falloff in asylum admissions after 2001, which prevented many of those who may have had legitimate claims from seeking refuge in the United States. In 2002, the number fell to less than half of the previous year, and only in 2008 recovered to pre-9/11 levels. Most of those who arrive in the United States seeking asylum for political or religious persecution are now routinely detained while their claims are being heard, a traumatic experience for individuals who so often are fleeing violence or abuse. In many cases asylum seekers are forced to wear prison uniforms, held in jails and jail-like facilities, and sometimes comingled with criminal inmates.[67] This detention policy has included families with small children.[68] The prisons are frequently in remote locations that make it difficult to gain access to legal counsel, which is often the difference between asylum claims being accepted or rejected.[69] Asylum seekers can be detained for months, and sometimes even years.[70]

Since changes to the law in 1996, asylum seekers also face the possibility of expedited removal, in which they can be immediately turned away if they fail to make a clear request for asylum or if they cannot persuade an asylum officer that they have a "credible fear" of persecution and do not request a judicial review. The expedited removal process applies to claimants who do not have travel documents or who have fraudulent ones. Although it is appropriate for immigration officers to have such authority, expedited removal needs to be exercised with caution to ensure that those who may face persecution if they are returned home are given an adequate hearing. A two-year study by the United States Commission on International Religious Freedom found that while proper procedures had been put in place at ports of entry, implementation varied considerably, and in a significant minority of cases individuals claiming fear of persecution had nonetheless immediately been removed to their home countries.[71]

Issues regarding the treatment of illegal immigrants and those seeking refuge in the United States are among the hardest faced by the officials responsible for making these decisions. Deportation is a harsh penalty that profoundly affects the lives of those removed, and many illegal immigrants have a strong incentive to avoid removal by whatever means possible. Genuine asylum seekers may face imprisonment or violence at home if they are denied entry by the United States. Finding the proper balance between upholding the law and ensuring due process is extremely important.

The Task Force believes that the United States needs to uphold the highest standards for due process and fair treatment of refugees, asylum seekers, and those facing deportation because they are living in the country illegally.

DEVELOPMENT

The United States has rarely thought about how its policies to encourage economic development in poorer countries might affect immigration; similarly, it has rarely thought about how its immigration policies might affect development. For a variety of historical and institutional reasons, the United States has generally separated economic development policy from immigration policy. This contrasts with Europe, where full membership in the European Union—which includes the right for citizens of one EU country to work in any other—has been conditional on reaching certain economic benchmarks. The EU strategy for admitting poorer member countries such as Greece, Spain, Portugal, and Poland was to invest large sums to bring living standards in those countries closer to the standards of the more advanced EU members. This was fairly successful with earlier entrants like Spain and Portugal, though less so in the case of newer members like Poland and the Baltic states, where the income discrepancies with western Europe were considerably larger.

Washington has encouraged developing countries that send large numbers of migrants to the United States—particularly Mexico and Central America—to pursue economic development through openness to trade and foreign investment, and has not offered much direct development aid. Trade agreements such as the North American Free Trade Agreement (NAFTA) and the Central American Free Trade Agreement (CAFTA) excluded most issues related to labor mobility, though some small categories of visa preferences were created for citizens of Canada and Mexico, as well as for Chile and Singapore, which have signed free trade agreements with the United States. Both the United States and Mexico have long been wary of the sacrifices to sovereignty involved in the European model of integration, and there is little likelihood of that changing in the near future. But there are nonetheless numerous possibilities for closer cooperation that might address some of the root causes of high levels of migration.

The Task Force believes that economic development inside the sending countries is the best way to discourage mass emigration. The difficulty of this task cannot be overestimated, however. The reality is that the sort of strong, steady growth necessary to reduce migratory pressures remains elusive in many countries. Although the European model has been successful in some respects, the disparities between the newer EU members and older ones were not nearly as large as the disparity between the United States and most of the countries that send large numbers of immigrants here.

A 1985 Council on Foreign Relations study that looked at the prospects for slowing northward migration from Latin America concluded that "development is not only uncertain; it is also a gradual process, with effects measured over . . . decades rather than [in] months and years. Thus even a successful development effort cannot be expected to have an impact on migration trends in the near future."[72] Further, most of what determines the success of development efforts in sending countries is not in the hands of the U.S. government. It depends largely on the internal governance in these countries, their educational systems, their resource bases, their tax and investment policies, and their attractiveness to international capital. The United States can have some influence on the policies pursued by these governments, but it is extremely limited. There is scope for more targeted U.S. efforts to encourage economic development, especially in Mexico. But the impact on emigration, particularly in the short term, is likely to be minimal.

A more promising prospect is for the United States to take a closer look at how its immigration policies can be used to encourage development in the sending countries. At its heart, development is about the reduction of poverty, and immigration can be an important component. As *The Economist* recently put it, "Migration has turned out to be a very successful strategy for the world's poor to make their lives a little bit better." The same economic opportunities that propelled so many European immigrants to cross the Atlantic Ocean in the nineteenth and early twentieth centuries are leading some in the world's developing nations to seek a new life in wealthier countries—from the Middle East to Europe to the United States.

The history of the last great migration showed that emigration was not antithetical to development in Europe. Indeed, it would be more accurate to say that emigration helped reduce economic pressures in Europe at a time of political and economic stress. Further, a surprisingly high percentage of those who emigrated from Europe to the New World (about one-third) eventually returned home. Today, this sort of circular migration is occurring on an unprecedented scale. Increasingly, some immigrants are splitting their time between their countries of birth and their adopted countries, rendering obsolete old notions that the emigration of highly skilled individuals necessarily results in a brain drain for developing countries. The development of India's vibrant information technology industry, for example, has been driven in large measure by Indian immigrants to the United States who have returned home to build businesses that take advantage of their knowledge of the U.S. market.

The most obvious measure of the economic benefits of migration to sending countries is remittances from those working in advanced countries, which have more than doubled over the past five years to more than $300 billion in 2008, though even this likely understates the size of total remittances. Latin Americans alone remitted about $66 billion in 2008. In certain countries, the contribution of remittances is enormous; they account for 25 percent of gross domestic product (GDP) in Honduras, for instance, and 20 percent in Jamaica. But there are more subtle benefits that are likely more important and lasting. Unlike the immigrants of a century ago, modern migrants can move more quickly and easily between their home and adopted countries, and can keep in close touch through modern communications.[73]

A major study carried out for the Public Policy Institute of California in 1999, for instance, found that highly skilled immigrants to the state, particularly in the technology sector, had spurred trade and investment linkages between the state and their home countries. The study found that immigrant entrepreneurs from Taiwan, China, and India in particular had created networks of professional and business ties between the United States and Asia. The result has been a significant contribution to economic development in both regions.[74] Indeed, there are some signs that—in part because of the hurdles for immigrants wanting to settle permanently in the United States and in part because of increased opportunities in places like China and India—a growing proportion of highly skilled immigrants are returning home, in what has been dubbed a reverse brain drain.[75] Another study has tried to quantify the trade effects of immigration, showing that over time a 10 percent increase in the number of immigrants a country sends to the United States will increase U.S. exports to that country by nearly 5 percent and imports by more than 8 percent.[76]

There are legitimate worries that creaming the best talent from developing countries could weaken the ability of those countries to develop their own economies, which is the only way for most of their citizens to escape poverty. There is no question that some countries, especially in Africa, face serious skills shortages. Ghana has just 6.2 doctors per hundred thousand people, and close to three-quarters of its doctors leave the country within a decade of gaining a medical degree. In five African countries, nearly half of the highly educated population lives abroad. Eight out of ten Haitians and Jamaicans with college degrees have left. But there are also examples where migration has produced positive incentives for sending countries to invest in educating skilled workers. The Philippines, for instance, which sends thousands of nurses around the world, has developed an impressive system for educating nurses to meet that demand; the result is that, though many trained nurses leave to work abroad, many have also stayed at home, leaving the country with more nurses per capita than Great Britain.[77]

The advantages of circular migration are not confined to the most highly skilled workers. There is evidence that seasonal agriculture workers returning home from Canada to Mexico are more likely to invest in land and small businesses, for instance, and similar trends have been shown among lower-skilled workers returning from the United States to El Salvador and the Dominican Republic.[78]

Overall, the Task Force finds that open immigration policies in the advanced countries, including the United States, strongly benefit the vast majority of sending countries in the developing world. This is certainly true for the individuals involved, because the welfare gains of emigrating to more advanced countries are so enormous. As Michael Clemens and Lant Pritchett have pointed out, roughly two of every five Mexicans who have escaped poverty, and four of every five Haitians, did so by leaving their countries. And the money that emigrants send back home has helped lift millions of others out of poverty.[79] *Although efforts to encourage economic development in sending countries are central, the Task Force finds that open immigration policies in the United States and other advanced countries are complementing development in poorer countries rather than detracting from it.*

MEXICO

Immigration is the most important issue in one of America's most important bilateral relationships, with its Mexican neighbor. For that reason alone, the United States needs to take a renewed look at the impact its immigration policies have beyond its borders.

For many in the United States, the immigration issue is almost entirely about Mexico, and not without some reason. Mexico is by far the largest source of immigrants to the United States, both those who come legally and those who come illegally, and it is the transit country for many immigrants from Central America, which is the second biggest source of undocumented migrants. About eleven million Mexicans represent more than 30 percent of the foreign-born population currently living in the United States. And the numbers have grown steadily in recent decades. As a share of Mexico's national population, the number of Mexican immigrants living in the United States was just 1.5 percent in 1970 but more than 10 percent in 2005.[80] In 2007, Mexicans living abroad, mostly in the United States, sent home approximately $24 billion in remittances.[81] The size of the migration flows from Mexico is enough to give it a central place in any discussion of broader U.S. immigration policies.

Since the enactment of NAFTA in 1994, the U.S. and Mexican economies have become ever more closely linked; some 85 percent of Mexico's exports come to the United States, and Mexico is the second largest market for U.S. exports after Canada. American companies provide more than 60 percent of all foreign direct investment in Mexico, and bilateral trade has tripled in the last two decades. As a result of this unique combination of large trade and migratory flows to the United States, Mexico has been most keenly and deeply affected by the choices the United States has made about immigration. Conversely, the United States has most keenly and deeply felt the impact of Mexican policies that have contributed to the vast northward migration, in particular that country's failure to lift its economy fast enough to provide enough jobs for its citizens at home.

Mexico, along with Canada, is also a vitally important part of U.S. homeland security policies aimed at keeping terrorists from carrying out another successful attack in the United States. The United States and Mexico have cooperated closely in trying to make certain that terrorist groups do not use Mexico as a transit route into this country. Some of the efforts on this front have not received much public attention, yet both Mexico and the United States have clearly recognized their strong common interest in counterterrorism initiatives. The Mexican government is acutely aware that, were there to be an attack in which terrorists used Mexico as a transit country to the United States, the inevitable U.S. reaction would be enormously damaging to Mexico's economy. The countries have also deepened their cooperation to deal with the huge and persistent problem of illegal drugs, which has spawned deadly violence on the Mexican side of the border as warring drug cartels have found themselves under greater pressure from the Mexican government. The administration of Mexican president Felipe Calderón has been willing to work more closely with the United States, including military-to-military cooperation, than any previous Mexican government. The United States in turn has pledged $1.4 billion in weapons and training under the Merida Initiative to help the Mexican government in its war with the drug cartels, though most of the promised assistance has yet to be disbursed. The Obama administration recently announced significant new efforts to stem the flow of cash and weapons from the United States to the cartels in Mexico, and has publicly acknowledged that the United States needs to step up efforts to reduce the demand for illegal drugs that is fueling the cartels.

The Task Force finds that Mexico represents a special case for U.S. immigration policy. Because of the size of the cross-border labor flows, its close economic integration with the United States, and the implications for U.S. homeland security, the U.S-Mexico relationship on migration issues is particularly important for American foreign policy interests.

Why has there been such large migration from Mexico to the United States, especially in the past three or four decades? Two developments are largely responsible: first, rapid population growth and comparatively modest economic growth in Mexico, and, second, high levels of economic inequality within Mexico and between Mexico and the United States. In addition, as migration from Mexico has increased, it has become easier for other immigrants to join relatives or friends already in the United States, a network effect that has encouraged additional migration.

The biggest single explanation for the large migration northward is the huge growth in Mexico's working-age population, and the failure of the Mexican economy to generate the rapid growth necessary to absorb those new workers. During the U.S. baby boom of the postwar period, birth rates in the two countries were similar, but after 1960 they diverged sharply. The result was a surge in emigration from Mexico beginning in the late 1970s, when Mexico's young working-age population continued to grow rapidly even as it was declining in the United States. Economists estimate that about one-third of total immigration from Mexico to the United States over the past four decades can be explained by higher Mexican birth rates.[82]

Those demographic pressures are beginning to ease. The birth rate in Mexico has fallen from nearly seven children per mother in the mid-1960s to just 2.2 today, barely above replacement rate and only slightly higher than the U.S. level of 2.1.[83] This is one of the fastest declines in fertility ever recorded in any nation. In the 1990s, when illegal migration from Mexico reached record levels, its working-age population was growing by one million each year; today that growth rate is just 500,000. Although the United States will continue to attract many Mexicans seeking higher wages and a better life, the population pressures of the past two decades are already starting to recede, and a reduction in the pressures to migrate to the United States will likely follow.[84]

The second reason for the high level of emigration has been the weakness of the Mexican economy. While Mexico is likely in the future to generate sufficient employment to keep more of its smaller working-age population at home, for the past several decades that has not been the case. Mexico's economy grew steadily in the 1960s and 1970s, but per capita GDP dropped sharply after the debt crisis of 1982, and never fully recovered. Differences in per capita income between Mexico and the United States did not narrow at all between 1980 and 2005, even as many developing countries in Asia and other parts of Latin America closed that gap. Mexican migration rates to the United States have been particularly high following shocks that produced recessions or slower growth in Mexico.[85] Since 2003, the rapid pace of trade growth with the United States has also slowed in the face of growing competition from China and other parts of the world. Immigration has been a safety valve for the underperforming Mexican economy; migration to the north has promised jobs to Mexicans when none were available at home. There are positive signs, however, even amidst the current global recession. Many U.S. and other foreign companies are continuing to expand their investments in Mexico, lured by the cost benefits of a weaker peso, the proximity to the U.S. market, and the fear of rising energy costs that make shipping from Asia less attractive.[86]

The economic gains in moving from Mexico to the United States are substantial. Immigration economist and Task Force member Gordon Hanson has estimated that migration to the United States would increase the wage of a typical twenty-five-year-old male with nine years of education from $2.30 per hour to $8.50 per hour, adjusting for cost-of-living differences.[87] Illegal migration from Mexico to the United States also appears to rise when the Mexican economy has been at its weakest relative to the U.S. economy. Apprehensions at the border—the primary measure the Department of Homeland Security uses to estimate illegal migration across the southern U.S. border—rose sharply, for instance, in 1983, 1987, and 1995. Each year corresponds to an economic crisis in Mexico. In 2008, with the deep recession in the United States, apprehensions at the border fell to their lowest level since the 1970s.[88] Historically, apprehensions have increased and decreased with seasonal employment patterns, indicating that some portion of the Mexican population working illegally in the United States moves back and forth across the border each year.[89]

NAFTA has brought many benefits for both the United States and Mexico, and for Mexico has produced a burgeoning export sector in industries that might otherwise have located in China or other parts of Asia. The reforms in the Mexican economy have also helped to build the conditions for stronger economic growth. In the shorter term, however, NAFTA probably exacerbated the illegal immigration problem as low-productivity farms or small manufacturing operations adapted by shedding labor and investing in technologies to improve productivity, or were forced out of business by competitive imports. Indeed, a high-level

FIGURE 4. BORDER APPREHENSIONS, 1966–2007*

*Includes administrative arrests by ICE.

Source: Department of Homeland Security, 2008.

commission on migration set up by Congress in the late 1980s recommended that opening trade with Mexico was the best way to encourage the economic development that would ultimately lessen migration pressures. But it predicted—accurately, as it turned out—that freer trade would increase illegal immigration to the United States in the short and medium term. The report noted that although "job-creating economic growth is the ultimate solution to reducing . . . migratory pressures, the economic development process itself tends in the short and medium term to stimulate migration by raising expectations and enhancing people's ability to migrate."[90] In terms of migration from Mexico, the story has not yet moved beyond the medium term.

The Task Force finds that, though some of the domestic conditions that have led to mass illegal migration from Mexico to the United States are likely to improve, migration pressures will remain significant unless Mexico's economy can grow more rapidly and create jobs for its working-age population.

Rapid migration from Mexico to the United States has also had a reinforcing dynamic. Once migrant communities have become well established, it is easier for family members, friends, and others to follow the path already laid down. This has been particularly the case since the 1986 Immigration Reform and Control Act (IRCA) that legalized close to three million unauthorized immigrants living in the United States, the majority of them Mexican. As those individuals acquired green cards and citizenship, they were able to sponsor family members to join them legally in the country.

Finally, increased U.S. border enforcement efforts, though necessary, have had the unintended effect of increasing the population of Mexican and Central American migrants living permanently but illegally in the United States. U.S. border enforcement began to increase substantially following the passage of the 1986 legislation. From 1993 to 2008, the budget for the U.S. Border Patrol, which is responsible for policing the border regions, has grown fourfold, and the number of agents has increased from fewer than 4,000 to nearly 20,000. Despite that massive investment in border enforcement, until recently such measures were doing little to slow the flow of illegal migrants across the border. Although a significant percentage of those trying to cross are apprehended by the Border Patrol, the only consequence in most cases is that they are returned across the border and simply try again. As a result, the vast majority of illegal border crossers eventually succeed and get through to the United States.[91] But once here, there are strong incentives to remain and not attempt another crossing. Additional enforcement has made border crossing difficult enough that most illegal migrants are forced to rely on immigrant smugglers, or coyotes, paying an average of more than $2,000 for passage into the United States (though by some estimates that cost has recently reached as high as $6,000). The trip is increasingly dangerous. At least 5,000 migrants have died since 1995 while attempting unauthorized crossings of the southwest border.

The result is that a higher percentage of migrants cannot risk a return trip to Mexico and end up remaining permanently in the United States. Once they decide to stay, many attempt to bring their families as well to avoid permanent separation, increasing the population of school-age children and others who receive taxpayer-supported education, health care, and other services.[92] By disrupting long-established patterns of circular migration across the border, U.S. enforcement efforts have had the unintended effect of contributing to increases in the settled population of unauthorized immigrants living permanently in the United States.

Illegal immigration from Mexico to the United States prompted the two governments to sit down in early 2001 to begin discussions on a bilateral migration accord that tried to bring some order into the chaotic border situation. Mexican president Vicente Fox and U.S. president George W. Bush agreed to set up a high-level commission to address bilateral migration issues. They agreed in principle to acknowledge migration as a shared problem and to find ways to cooperate to make it more orderly, humane, and legal.[93] The talks were focused on several issues identified as critical by a bilateral expert commission headed by Thomas F. McLarty III, former White House chief of staff and special envoy for the Americas, and co-chair of this Task Force, and Andrés Rozental, former deputy foreign minister of Mexico. These included improving treatment for Mexican migrants by making legal visas more accessible, reducing unauthorized migration by cracking down on criminal smuggling organizations on both sides of the border, and targeting joint development initiatives on regions of high emigration from Mexico.

Despite seriousness and good faith, the talks never made significant progress on the most politically difficult issues for each side: for the United States, whether it would legalize unauthorized Mexican migrants already living in the country; and, for Mexico, whether it would take steps to discourage emigration to the United States. And the negotiations effectively came to a halt after the 9/11 terrorist attacks. The question of whether to revive efforts at such a bilateral accord is a critical one still facing both countries. Given the failed talks, Mexico is unlikely to propose a similar negotiation unless it has clearer signs that the U.S. Congress is moving forward on immigration reform. From the U.S. perspective, immigration reform is likely to be easier politically without such a negotiation; there are many reasons for the United States to move ahead on its own, without the complication of a new bilateral negotiation with Mexico. But the improvements in the U.S.-Mexico relationship offer hopeful possibilities for joint efforts to better manage migration and border issues in the future.

The Need for Comprehensive Immigration Reform

The task of making U.S. immigration policies better serve America's national interests is an urgent one facing the current administration and Congress. The previous section covered six major dimensions of America's foreign policy strongly influenced by its immigration policies: the economy, national security, public diplomacy, American values, development policy, and the vital relationship with Mexico. Crafting and implementing immigration policies that will better serve these interests requires both a major legislative initiative and a series of incremental changes designed to make the immigration system function more smoothly and effectively.

It has been said many times before, but it is also the conclusion of this Task Force that the current immigration system is badly broken. It will take both changes to the law and changes to current practices to make the system function more effectively. *The Task Force recommends that a new effort to pass a comprehensive immigration reform bill be a first-tier priority for the Obama administration and Congress, and that such an effort be restarted without delay. The Task Force is encouraged by the early signs from the administration that immigration reform is high on the agenda and that efforts will begin promptly to move ahead with legislation. But reforming immigration laws is not enough. At the same time, the United States needs to invest in making the immigration system operate more effectively.*

Congress has tried repeatedly to address some of the problems in the immigration system, passing significant legislation in 1986, 1990, and 1996. Yet the conclusions of the congressionally established Jordan Commission in 1994 remain as true today as they were then. "Serious problems undermine present immigration policies, their implementation, and their credibility: people who should get in find a cumbersome process that often impedes their entry; people who should not get in find it all too easy to enter; and people who are here without permission remain with impunity."[94]

The Bush administration and Congress made efforts to overhaul U.S. immigration laws in 2006 and 2007, but in the face of strong opposition from both sides of the debate, a compromise could not be found. By some measures, Congress was not far from a deal, and there would seem to be reasonable grounds for another effort. The final vote in the Senate in 2007, for instance, fell only seven votes short of the sixty-vote majority needed to end debate and bring the bill to a final vote. But by other measures, the differences that led to the failure in Congress remain significant, and compromise will not easily be reached. Although there was considerable support for the 2007 Senate bill, little of it was enthusiastic, with many backers considering it only marginally preferable to the status quo. In addition, opponents of the legislation were strong and vocal in their denunciations. And, though the principles of the congressional proposals were generally sound, by the time of its eventual defeat, the Senate bill had become so complex that effective implementation by the Department of Homeland Security and other agencies would likely have been impossible. *The Task Force believes that the administration and Congress must be careful that a legislative reform effort does not simply impose a huge additional mandate on an already over-burdened bureaucracy. It is not enough to pass comprehensive immigration reform; this time, reform must work.* Further, even if a compromise can be reached, the United States must break out of the pattern in which Congress revisits immigration policy every decade or so, approves what is claimed at the time to be a lasting fix, and then washes its hands of the issue until the problems again become too big to ignore.

Since 2007, the administration's primary response to the failure of comprehensive immigration reform has been to escalate enforcement at the border and to toughen measures to stop companies from employing unauthorized migrants. In an effort to keep out illegal immigrants, the United States has expanded the Border Patrol into the nation's largest law enforcement agency, spent billions on deploying high-tech virtual barriers, and is close to completing construction of nearly seven hundred miles of pedestrian and vehicle fences along its southern border with Mexico. It has boosted enforcement at the work site, both through efforts to discourage hiring of unauthorized workers and selective raids at companies that continue to employ many such individuals.

Although many in the media, and some in Congress, continue to insist that U.S. borders are out of control and insecure, the Task Force believes that the border enforcement efforts of the past several years are impressive

and not well enough understood by the public. The number of Border
Patrol agents, for instance, grew from fewer than 3,000 before the 1986
immigration reform law to more than 9,000 by the end of the century,
a significant increase. But since 2005, that number has again almost
doubled, from just over 10,000 agents to nearly 20,000, an enormous
increase that underscored the high priority given to border security in
the second term of the Bush administration. After some early growing pains, the Department of Homeland Security is moving ahead
with the deployment of video cameras and other sensing devices along
the southwest border that will help target enforcement efforts by the
Border Patrol, which is particularly important in remote regions staffed
by fewer agents. Along with increased border enforcement, DHS last
year removed nearly 350,000 illegal immigrants apprehended inside the
United States, a 20 percent increase over 2007 and by far the highest

FIGURE 5. ALIENS REMOVED, 1980–2007

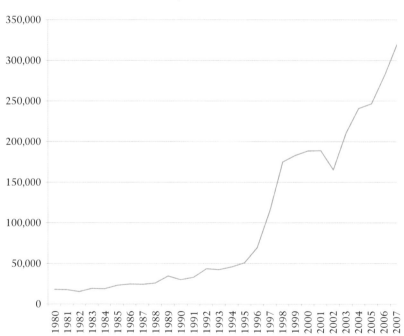

Source: Department of Homeland Security *Yearbook of Immigration Statistics*, 2007.

FIGURE 6. NUMBER OF BORDER PATROL AGENTS, 1980–2008

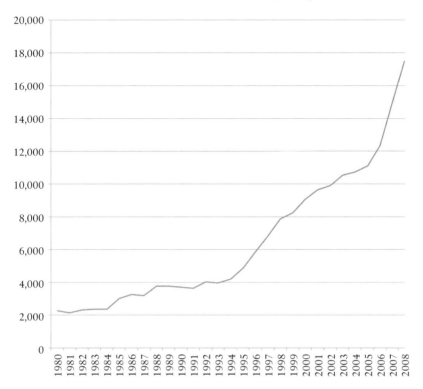

Sources: 1980–2005 data from Syracuse University Transitional Records Access Clearinghouse on Immigration; 2005–2008 data from the Department of Homeland Security.

number on record. The United States has also used intelligence gathering and modern technologies to help target terrorists, criminals, and others it wants to exclude from the country.[95]

The Task Force finds that these measures represent determined, expansive efforts to control America's borders and enforce U.S. immigration laws. But no amount of enforcement can eliminate the underlying problem, which is that aggressively enforcing a broken regime does not fix it. Unless the United States has a more sensible and efficient system for admitting legal migrants who come to take advantage of work opportunities, no reasonable level of enforcement is likely to be enough to resolve the illegal immigration problem.

As former secretary of homeland security Michael Chertoff put it, "When you try to fight economic reality, it is at best an extremely expensive and very, very difficult process and almost always doomed to failure."[96] *The Task Force believes that U.S. immigration laws are enforced poorly not because of inadequate funding or a refusal to take tough measures, but because they are overly complex and unenforceable as a practical matter. Until the United States can reform the immigration regime to bring it more in line with economic realities, enforcement will remain an uphill struggle.*

Comprehensive immigration reform is likely to be no easier in the current Congress than it was in the previous one. In some ways, it could be harder because the deep recession in the U.S. economy will leave many lawmakers with little appetite for measures aimed at making it easier for foreigners to come and work legally in the United States. But there may also be a window of opportunity. Although millions of illegal immigrants are still in the United States, the number trying to enter is falling rapidly, due to a combination of economic weakness and tougher enforcement. The construction industry, for example, which has employed many unauthorized migrants, was one of the earliest sectors hit by the economic downturn. Illegal immigrants are also easier for employers to dismiss, and thus tend to be the first let go as the economy weakens.[97] It is too soon to know whether illegal immigrants are returning home in large numbers, but there is no question that illegal migration to the United States has slowed significantly. By the best estimates available, the total number of illegal immigrants living in the United States began to decline in 2007, and may have already fallen by as many as 500,000.[98] Although a recession is never an easy time to consider reforming immigration laws, the decline in illegal immigration has the benefit of allowing Congress and the administration to focus on the broader set of issues raised in this report and elsewhere, rather than solely on the issue of controlling illegal immigration. In addition, it is critical that the U.S. government do everything it can to speed up the economic recovery and set the stage for future growth. An effective immigration system that provides timelier processing for immigrant workers who will be needed as the economy returns to growth is a critical component of the larger economic recovery package.

There are improvements to the immigration system that can and should be undertaken without legislation, but a piecemeal effort at reform is unlikely to make anything other than modest progress, given the flaws in the current legal regime and the complexity of the competing interests and concerns.

In this chapter, the report will discuss the four central elements of any immigration reform effort: improvements in the legal immigration system, more effective enforcement to discourage illegal immigration, a plan for dealing with those already living illegally in this country, and, finally, a strategy for ensuring successful integration of the growing number of immigrants who are arriving and settling in the United States.

ENCOURAGING LEGAL IMMIGRATION

Most immigrants come to the United States to work. They come here because wages, working conditions, and the prospects for a better life are far superior to what they find in their own countries. Migration is a wrenching experience, and the possibilities for gain must be significant before most people will take that leap. For illegal migrants, because of the greater risks they face, the benefits must be higher still.

As is being demonstrated by the current recession, the quickest way to discourage illegal migration is to stop creating jobs for migrants and everyone else. When the economy recovers, the demand for new immigrants, whether legal or illegal, will also recover. The current slowdown, therefore, should be seen as an opportunity to overhaul U.S. immigration policies to better serve U.S. economic needs as the economy regains its footing.

It is the view of the Task Force that getting legal immigration right is the most critical immigration policy challenge facing the administration and Congress. Although not enough on its own, the most effective way to combat illegal immigration is to have an immigration policy that provides adequate and timely means for the United States to admit legal immigrants.

Three central principles should guide the reform of the legal immigration system: first, the United States should be admitting immigrants (and their close family members) in the number and range of skills that reflect the demands from its economy; second, it needs a much simpler and more transparent system for admitting both migrants and temporary workers; and finally, the government must invest in making the legal immigration system work more efficiently.

IMMIGRANT NUMBERS

The current immigration system does not respond well to supply and demand in the U.S. labor market. Economics should not be the only factor shaping American immigration policy decisions, but neither can the United States simply ignore the vast economic forces that drive international migration. The effort to gain control of illegal migration is certain to fail unless the supply of foreign workers and the demand for them in the United States are brought more closely into line. That for much of this decade roughly 800,000 migrants could come to the United States illegally each year and find jobs is a clear indicator that the legal migration system has not remotely reflected market demand. Indeed, one of the reasons illegal immigration is so attractive not only to the migrants but also to U.S. employers is that it responds quickly to market pressures. The lengthy waits and substantial expense required for hiring most foreign workers through existing legal channels have discouraged many employers from using those channels, except for the most highly skilled workers.[99]

Labor market needs currently get far too little attention in deciding who gets priority to immigrate. For the past half century, most new immigrants coming to the United States have been family members of legal migrants or U.S. citizens. In 2008, nearly 700,000 people acquired green cards on the basis of family ties. By contrast, only just over 166,000 did so on the basis of employment, 76,000 to the employees and the remaining 90,000 to their spouses and children.[100] There has long been a debate over whether the strong preference for family reunification in U.S. immigration law serves American interests. There are clearly some good reasons for maintaining the policy—the family is a core unit of American society, and strong families are critical for the education, financial support, and social integration of newcomers to the country. Families can also serve as an information network, alerting relatives at home to job prospects in the United States, and providing them with support after they arrive. In addition, Congress created an income test in 1996 for those wishing to sponsor family members, and barring those family members from welfare or other forms of public assistance when they arrive. As a result, there are strong additional incentives for recent immigrants to work hard and save to meet the income requirements needed to sponsor family members to join them.

The current system for family-based immigration, however, is exceedingly slow, and does not work well even in bringing families together. As a result of quotas designed to limit immigrants from a handful of countries such as Mexico, India, and China, waits for sponsoring family members can stretch to a decade or more. The current backlog for adult siblings from the Philippines, for instance, is more than twenty years—so long that the applicant may well have finished most of his or her working life before arriving in the United States. For an adult child from Mexico, the waits are more than fifteen years. Even the waiting times for spouses and minor children of legal immigrants from anywhere in the world are often more than five years—a delay that is so long as to make a mockery of the concept of family reunification.

However, the system for admitting immigrants with needed skills but without family connections is even worse. Changes to the quotas as part of the 1990 Immigration Act raised the number of green cards for employment-based immigrants and their families from 56,000 to 140,000, but this remains a fraction of the numbers available for family members. In addition, most of the employment-based slots are claimed by individuals already living in the United States under some sort of temporary status. At the higher-skilled end, the main temporary visa available for bringing skilled workers to the United States and putting them on a path to permanent residence has been the H-1B visa program, though that same program has also been used heavily by Indian companies bringing over strictly temporary workers to support their business model of outsourcing back-office work for U.S. companies. American high technology companies are the main users of the H-1B program, although universities and other educational institutions as well as financial services companies are also significant employers. In 1999, as hiring in the technology industry was growing rapidly, Congress increased the annual quota for H-1B workers from 65,000 to 115,000 for 1999 and 2000, and then again raised it to 195,000 for the fiscal years 2001 to 2003. Unfortunately, the latter increase coincided with the collapse of the technology stock bubble, and came into effect just as employment in the industry was falling. Congress therefore let the cap revert to 65,000 in FY2004, just as the industry was beginning to recover. The result was that for several years the annual quota for H-1B workers was filled almost immediately; a 2005 fix by Congress to add twenty thousand slots for advanced degree holders helped only slightly. With the current recession, demand for H-1B workers has dropped, making the cap temporarily less of an impediment for U.S. companies, but it is clear that the quota is inadequate in anything but a deep recession.

The logic of the current quotas is that hiring more foreign technology workers will mean fewer jobs for American technology workers. There

TABLE 3. *TOP TWENTY COMPANIES—MOST H1-B VISA PETITION APPROVALS IN 2008*

Rank	Company	Approved Petitions
1	Infosys Technologies Ltd.	4,559
2	Wipro Ltd.	2,678
3	Satyam Computer Services Ltd.	1,917
4	Tata Consultancy Services Ltd.	1,539
5	Microsoft Corporation	1,037
6	Accenture LLP	731
7	Cognizant Technology Solutions Corporation	467
8	Cisco Systems Inc.	422
9	Larsen & Toubro Infotech Ltd.	403
10	IBM India Private Limited	381
11	Intel Corporation	351
12	Ernst & Young LLP	321
13	Patni Americas Inc.	296
14	Terra Infotech Inc.	281
15	Qualcomm Incorporated	255
16	MPhasiS Corporation	251
17	KPMG LLP	245
18	Prince George's County Public Schools	239
19	Baltimore City Public School System	229
20	Deloitte Consulting LLP	218

Source: U.S. Citizenship and Immigration Services, 2009.

is little evidence, however, that those restrictions end up creating more jobs for American workers. Indeed, the opposite is likely the case. More than 90 percent of Google employees, for instance, are Americans, yet the company last year was able to get only half the H-1B workers it had sought. Google argues that "if we're to remain an innovative company—one that is creating jobs in the U.S. every day—we also need to hire exceptional candidates who happen to have been born elsewhere. After all, if we were to hire only U.S.-born talent, we would effectively close ourselves off from most of the world's population." Microsoft recently decided to open a new research facility across the border in Vancouver, Canada, rather than in Washington State, citing its inability to bring skilled foreign workers into the United States. The result will be more jobs for Canadian workers, and fewer for Americans. A recent survey by the National Venture Capital Association found that one-third of privately held venture capital-backed U.S. companies—the most innovative firms in the United States—had been increasing hiring abroad due to restrictions that prevented them from hiring foreign workers in this country.[101]

A number of other advanced industrialized nations have implemented policies that explicitly target immigrants whose skills the government believes are valuable to the economy, or are thought to be in short supply. Canada, Britain, Australia, and New Zealand all have what are known as points-based systems for selecting immigrants. They use factors such as education, occupation, work experience, age, and language skills to decide which immigrants to admit. The system is implemented by the government, in contrast to the U.S. scheme, which depends more on private companies identifying and hiring particular foreign workers.

In 2007, in the final throes of the debate over immigration reform, the Senate introduced a compromise bill crafted by senators Jon Kyl (R-AZ) and Edward Kennedy (D-MA) that would have introduced a points system in the United States. At the same time, it would have increased the percentage of employment-based green cards significantly and reduced family preferences, particularly for parents and siblings. The proposal generated strong opposition from many immigrant rights groups, who objected to the reduction in family preferences. But it also drew surprisingly strong hostility from business, which feared it would compromise the ability of companies to seek out and hire the best foreign workers and would instead place greater authority in the hands of the government.[102] The danger of a points system is that it can become delinked from the actual labor market, bringing in employment-based workers for whom no employment actually exists. Despite the arguments in favor of a points system, the United States, under its current system, has been the most successful country in the world in attracting the most highly skilled immigrants—a record that calls for reforming the current system to make it more efficient, easier to use, and more responsive to market demand, rather than adopting a different system wholesale.

U.S. policies for attracting low-skilled workers have also been divorced from the realities of supply and demand. The current legal quota for green cards for unskilled laborers and their families, for example, is just ten thousand each year, a miniscule number that does not begin to reflect actual demand. The H-2A visa program for temporary agricultural workers tends to be underused by employers because of its cost and complexity, whereas the H-2B program for seasonal workers has a quota that is normally too low to meet demand. In addition, there are restrictions that make it impossible for some employers with a legitimate need for nonseasonal temporary workers to qualify. There has also been little consistency in the scope and administration of either program. Congress allowed changes to the H-2B program, for instance, which had allowed returning temporary workers not to be counted against annual quotas, to expire at the end of 2007, which effectively cut the program in half. In a 2008 letter to congressional leaders that was signed by three governors, including former Arizona governor and current DHS secretary Janet Napolitano, the Western Governors Association said that the shortage of H-2B visas and the bureaucratic hurdles for the H-2A program "have created critical problems for key western business and industry."[103]

There has long been serious consideration given to expanding temporary worker programs, especially for low-skilled migrants from Mexico who would otherwise be likely to enter the United States illegally. A temporary worker program was a central feature of the failed immigration reform efforts in both 2006 and 2007. Temporary and seasonal work programs have been the only mechanism that has allowed the cross-border flow of workers from Mexico to the United States to be funneled into a program that can be monitored by government authorities. The biggest dilemma has been how to enforce labor certification, minimum wage, and labor rights provisions in an effort to ensure that migrant workers are not being exploited, and are not used by employers to drive down wages and standards for American workers. The existing H-2A program for agricultural guest workers, as noted, is underused because farm employers consider it too onerous, especially given the number of readily available unauthorized workers. Only about 75,000 of a labor force estimated at 2.5 million are admitted each year under the program. Yet changes made in the final weeks of the Bush administration, though they would make it easier for employers to use the H-2A program, have been criticized for weakening many of the protections for workers. (The Obama administration has delayed implementation of the regulations until the end of the year.)[104]

Temporary worker programs have never been a panacea, and the U.S. experience with such schemes has been decidedly mixed. The biggest of these was the Bracero Program for Mexican agricultural workers. Initially designed as a temporary measure to deal with wartime labor shortages, it became an established guest worker program after World War II, with the number of legal workers reaching 445,000 in 1956. The program, however, became notorious for widespread labor rights abuses and was shut down by Congress in 1965. The scheme is seen as having led to a sizable increase in the number of guest workers who settled permanently in the United States as illegal immigrants.[105]

The United States is not alone in its mixed experiences. Other countries have generally been unsuccessful in creating smoothly functioning guest worker programs[106] for at least two reasons. First, except in certain industries, such as agriculture and tourism, which have large seasonal employment fluctuations, temporary work is something of a misnomer. Many temporary work permits are for full-time, year-round jobs, but with the assumption that at the end of a certain period, usually three years, the individual will return home. The assumption collides with too much of what is known about human nature and economic realities. Someone who leaves home for three years almost invariably puts down some roots in the new community, and is unlikely to leave voluntarily at the end of that period. The employee may have come to depend on the higher wage, much of which is often sent back home to families as remittances. An employer may also be reluctant to lose a good employee. The tendency to stay on in the host country is particularly strong if job opportunities back home are few, which is almost always the case, given that unemployment or underemployment at home is what drives most individuals abroad in the first place. As a result, many temporary workers try to find legal channels to remain permanently in their adopted countries or, failing that, often remain illegally.

The second problem is that the conditions of employment for temporary workers tend to be substandard, with employers sometimes paying workers below the legal minimum wage and withholding normal employment benefits. In cases where an individual's legal status in the host country depends on a particular job, as is frequently the case, those workers have little or no ability to seek better wages or working conditions. Unions have found it particularly difficult, and usually impossible, to organize foreign workers enrolled in such programs. The United States has attempted to deal with these criticisms by requiring that employers attest that they have been unable to find enough workers domestically, and that they will offer foreign workers the same wages and working conditions as domestic employees. But in practice such labor certification requirements have been extremely difficult to enforce, particularly with the inadequate resources devoted to the task.

COMPLEXITY

The current legal immigration system is inordinately complex and cumbersome. Lengthy delays in processing routine requests make it difficult, if not impossible, to carry out an immigration policy that serves the nation's interests. According to the U.S. Citizenship and Immigration Services (USCIS) ombudsman, many of the "pervasive and serious problems" in the handling of legal immigration and visa claims "stem from the complexity and opaque nature of the immigration rules and the agency administering them."[107] The basic law underlying U.S. immigration policy was written in 1952, and since that time most of the changes approved by Congress have simply layered additional burdens on an already inadequate law and an ineffective bureaucracy. In addition, there are a myriad of other laws, policies, memoranda, and guidelines that are relevant to many different aspects of the visa and immigration process. As the USCIS ombudsman has put it, the system is "a hodgepodge of disconnected, overlapping, and contradictory rules."[108]

What the United States should have is a clear, disciplined, transparent, and flexible system. A clear system would be one in which the rules are well known and easily understandable to anyone who wishes to immigrate or to come here temporarily for study or work. Instead, the system is so complex that it is virtually impossible to navigate without an immigration lawyer, and even then mistakes get made and can be extremely costly. Even immigration inspectors and adjudicators frequently make mistakes, creating substantial downstream work in correcting the errors. A disciplined system would be one in which decisions are timely and predictable. Instead, virtually every part of the process—from the initial visa application to naturalization as a U.S. citizen—is characterized by lengthy delays. A transparent system would be one in which it is easy for applicants to obtain the information they need on the requirements for applications. Instead, there is no single source for basic information about U.S. immigration laws, and their related processes and policies, and it is difficult for individuals to track the status of their applications. A flexible system would be one in which immigration levels adjust more easily to the state of the economy. Instead, much of the legal immigration system is largely impervious to economic conditions in the United States.

This complexity has evolved largely as a result of many years of makeshift fixes to specific problems, but it has reached the point where those ad hoc adjustments have created a dysfunctional system. There are, for example, some two dozen categories of visas allowing temporary admission to the United States, and more than seventy-five subcategories, covering everyone from athletes to criminal informants to temporary employees from Chile and Singapore who receive special treatment as a result of U.S. trade agreements with those countries. Although each of the categories may be defensible on its own, the collective result is hopelessly unwieldy. According to the Migration Policy Institute's comprehensive 2006 Independent Task Force on Immigration and America's Future, "The chaotic nature of immigration rules represents a true public policy danger in that the system invites manipulation by potential workers and employers, ad hoc fixes by policymakers, and widespread loss of confidence from the public."[109]

Although it will never be easy to simplify a system that must deal with such a huge volume and diversity of individual cases, the Task Force believes that the government must begin moving in that direction. For more than half a century, the United States has made the system more and more complicated; it is time to begin reversing course.

The current template for legal immigration to the United States also bears little resemblance to how most immigration actually takes place. The assumption on which the laws are written is that most aspiring immigrants will apply from their home countries for permission to immigrate to the United States, and then wait their turn in line. That may once have been an accurate reflection of the reality, but currently most who immigrate permanently to the United States spend many years living here first on some kind of temporary visa.

In theory, almost everyone who comes to the United States on a temporary visa—whether as a tourist, a student, or an employee—is expected to demonstrate the intent to return home after the visa expires. Temporary visa holders who fail to do so can be barred from entering or from returning if they have traveled abroad. Yet in practice, the distinction between temporary employees and permanent immigrants has utterly broken down. Because permanent visas are so difficult to obtain, temporary ones have become a substitute. Far more temporary work visas are therefore issued each year than employment-based green cards. In 2008, for instance, more than 166,000 employment-based green cards were issued to both employees and their family members; in comparison, more than 600,000 temporary work visas were issued, many to people living in the United States for years and waiting for a green card. More than 60 percent of those seeking green cards each year are already in the United States; that figure is nearly 90 percent for employment-based immigrants.[110]

There are good arguments in favor of an immigration system that allows many people to come here first on some sort of temporary basis. The process permits a potential immigrant to experience living and working in the United States before making the more consequential decision to immigrate. The student visa program, for instance, has been an enormously important channel for attracting young, highly skilled individuals who often end up living permanently in the United States. On the demand side, temporary schemes are also easier for the government to adjust upward and downward as economic conditions in the United States change, a flexibility that does not exist with family-based permanent immigration.

Yet the system as it currently operates, though it has many merits, is undermined by complex rules and the restrictions imposed by quotas and processing delays, all of which end up leaving many individuals who would like to seek permanent residence stuck for years as temporary workers. Their uncertain status creates real hardships for these individuals (for instance, spouses of most temporary visa holders are not permitted to work) and uncertainties for their employers. The result at best is widespread resentment of a system that forces these individuals to live in a kind of second-class status for many years; at

FIGURE 7. TEMPORARY WORKER ADMISSIONS VERSUS
GREEN-CARD ISSUANCES, 1998–2008

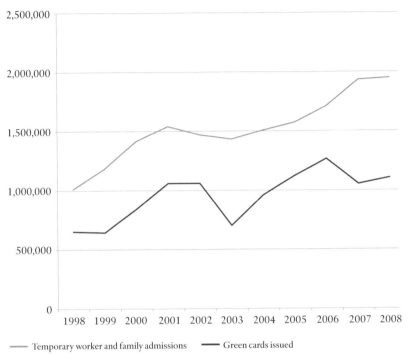

——— Temporary worker and family admissions   ▬▬ Green cards issued

Source: Department of Homeland Security *Yearbook of Immigration Statistics,* 2009.

worst, they simply pick up and leave, as growing numbers appear to be doing.[111] The Canadian province of Alberta, for instance, has advertised its eagerness to lure away U.S. temporary visa holders who have been unable to convert to permanent status, offering quick approval of permanent residence for skilled workers in certain occupations.[112] In simplifying the immigration system, the United States needs to move to a scheme that more closely resembles how migration actually occurs in the world today.

GOVERNMENT INVESTMENT

Even if the current system can be simplified, it will not work properly without a more effective funding system for facilitating legal immigration. *The Task Force finds that some of the recent operational problems in the U.S. legal immigration system are a result of the way in which the system is financed.* The clearest indicator of the need for reform in the way we fund legal immigration services is the long delay—frequently measured in years—for resolving many applications. Backlogs and delays have been historic, long-standing problems with the U.S. immigration system and have so far been immune to any lasting solution. For some, this is simply a nuisance; for others, the costs are extraordinarily high. A processing delay can prevent people from voting, bar them from working, or threaten their ability to remain in the United States if their temporary visa status expires before their immigrant visa application has been approved.

Congress has mandated that USCIS be self-funded. Under the current system, the cost of immigration processing is paid for entirely by a series of fees levied on visa applicants, temporary immigrants, green-card applicants, and those seeking U.S. citizenship. Certain types of visa applications are particularly expensive. Companies seeking to recruit an H-1B high-skilled worker, for example, can expect to pay between $5,000 and $6,000 in government fees and legal costs for each employee. The fees that must be paid directly to the government range from about $1,500 to more than $3,000, depending on the size of the company and the speed of processing it desires for an application.

The fee system has provided an important, stable source of funding for USCIS; before 1988, those fees had gone into the U.S. Treasury, and immigration services were often starved for funding. User funding for processing costs is a good model in principle: it places the burden on immigrants who stand to benefit substantially from coming to the United States and produces an increase in funding as the number of applications increases. But the way in which the fee structure operates has also contributed to many of the inefficiencies in the processing of immigration benefit applications. In particular, there has been a built-in incentive for green-card applications to be processed slowly because USCIS derives a considerable portion of its revenue from temporary employment authorization cards, which normally must be renewed annually. Those revenues are vital to the agency's budget, yet processing those claims takes personnel away from adjudicating permanent immigrant claims.

Reports by the USCIS ombudsman over the past several years have laid out the funding problems in detail and called for a range of needed responses. There are some encouraging signs. In 2007, the fees for green-card applications were boosted significantly to a level that will also finance the various interim work authorization benefits that many applicants require while awaiting adjudication. That has eliminated a big incentive for delays. Premium fees for faster processing—though they would ideally be unnecessary—have also provided a significant funding boost.

But the funding issues for immigration benefits highlight a more fundamental problem. Although the U.S. government has substantially boosted spending on immigration enforcement since DHS was created, this has been less the case for USCIS, the DHS agency responsible for dealing with immigrant, nonimmigrant, and naturalization applications. Government spending on the enforcement of immigration laws has increased dramatically, rising fivefold to more than $5 billion between 1985 and 2002. Since the 9/11 attacks, it has tripled again to more than $15 billion. The budget increases for USCIS have been far more modest, from $1.5 billion when DHS was created to $2.7 billion in 2009. In particular, because a substantial portion of USCIS work has been contracted out, staffing levels for government employees doing the critical work of adjudication have not kept pace with demand.[113] All the funding for USCIS comes from fees paid by immigrants, whereas enforcement is paid for from general congressional appropriations.

The underlying message is that America as a country believes that immigration serves only the interests of immigrants, and therefore they should pay the entire cost themselves. Further, the refusal to use any taxpayer money to pay for immigration services indicates that the United States does not believe that facilitating legal immigration is a significant national priority. One of the consequences is that USCIS is simply not held to the same accountability and performance standards by Congress as are other functions of the U.S. government, including immigration enforcement, which are paid for by taxpayers. *The Task Force believes that both facilitating legal immigration and preventing unlawful entry should be considered equally important priorities, and should receive the funding and oversight to ensure they perform at an optimal level.*

In particular, Congress should be prepared to appropriate funds to support the development of a modern infrastructure for processing immigrant and temporary visa applications. USCIS has recently launched a long-overdue Transformation Initiative to create a paperless processing system that should improve efficiency and customer service as it reduces fraudulent applications and speeds security

FIGURE 8. TOTAL BUDGETARY AUTHORITY BY ORGANIZATION:
CBP, ICE, AND USCIS

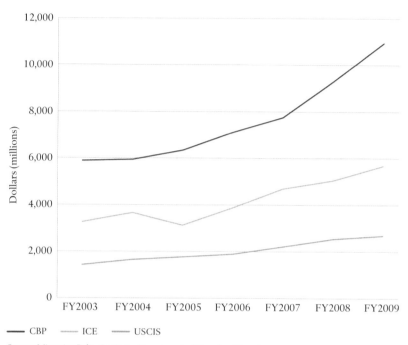

Sources: Migration Policy Institute; Department of Homeland Security, 2009.

checks. Although USCIS is budgeting to fund the initiative out of fee
revenue, infrastructure investment cannot be a single initiative, but
requires ongoing budgetary support.

Even with additional investments, there are no easy solutions to the
problem of processing delays. Given the number of applications that
must be considered each year, USCIS faces a herculean task, and one
that is far from predictable. Applications can surge for reasons that are
quite outside the agency's control, as they did in the early 1990s following Congress's 1986 decision to legalize nearly three million unauthorized migrants living in the country. Or they can surge more predictably,
as with the flood in citizenship applications in the summer of 2007 in
advance of the fee increase and a year before a presidential election.
Since 9/11, USCIS has been expected to allow time for exhaustive security background checks on applicants for green cards and citizenship.

FIGURE 9. FULL-TIME EMPLOYEES BY ORGANIZATION:
CBP, ICE, AND USCIS

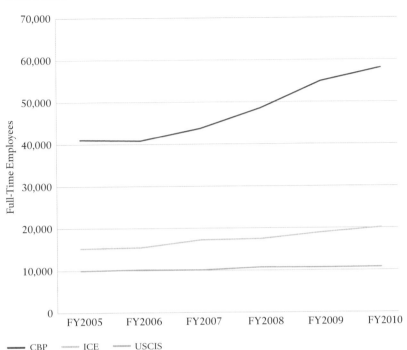

Sources: Migration Policy Institute; Department of Homeland Security, 2009.

These include a name check, which is carried out by the Federal Bureau of Investigation (FBI), and can involve searches of paper records that may be held at any one of 265 local FBI offices around the country. The security checks, and particularly the name checks, have introduced another often lengthy delay into the process, though the FBI has recently made impressive progress in reducing those delays by adding resources to allow background checks to be completed in a more timely fashion. Those efforts should be continued.[114] There have been other encouraging signs of progress. In the past fiscal year, for instance, USCIS reduced the average processing time for citizenship applications nearly in half, to roughly nine months, yet processed a record 1.17 million applications. The backlog of individuals awaiting FBI security clearances was also reduced significantly as a result of a substantial increase in the number of processors combined with better filtering of applicants.[115]

Despite the scale of the task, additional funds and a more stable funding structure are a necessary part of any sustainable solution.

DISCOURAGING ILLEGAL IMMIGRATION

The United States has the right, and the duty, to control and secure its borders. It is an affront to the rule of law that hundreds of thousands of people each year can enter the country unannounced or pose as visitors when their intention is to live here permanently. It is also true that, except for the small percentage who come here as drug smugglers or with the intention of committing other crimes, the vast majority of illegal immigrants have broken the law only in pursuit of a dream shared by many, to make better lives for themselves and for their families. But a central feature of the American dream is the idea that success comes from playing by the rules; that so many who wish to come here now try to succeed by violating the rules is a sad distortion of that ideal. *The Task Force believes that in any effort to reform immigration laws, the rule of law must be reasserted. No reform will be accepted by the American people, nor should it be, unless it restores respect for the law.* This means that alongside reform of its legal immigration system, the United States must assert greater control over its borders, assure compliance with terms of admission, and sharply reduce the number of jobs available to persons not authorized to work in this country.

Comprehensive immigration reform would substantially lower the flow of illegal migrants by providing alternative legal channels for migrants to live and work in the United States. That itself would be a big step toward gaining control of the border. Immigration reform would remove the hundreds of thousands of otherwise law-abiding individuals who are now coming to the United States to work illegally, so that U.S. enforcement efforts could focus more effectively on keeping out foreign terrorists, criminals, and others who pose a serious threat. Reducing the flow would also allow for a much higher apprehension rate, which would in turn discourage others who might be thinking about trying to enter the United States illegally. There is a law enforcement tipping point at which the costs and difficulty of entering illegally would become a powerful disincentive, particularly given the existence of new legal options. The sharp reduction in illegal entry into the United States over the past two years as the economy has softened and enforcement has grown indicates that it is possible to reach this tipping point in a recession; the challenge is to do so when the economy recovers and the demand for new employees again rises.

The Task Force believes that an effective enforcement regime centers on three elements: first, a comprehensive and accurate system that discourages employers from hiring unauthorized migrants; second, tougher enforcement at the borders that stops those who should not be admitted at a U.S. land border or port of entry; and, third, closer cooperation among federal, state, and local law enforcement officials in enforcing immigration laws.

EMPLOYMENT ENFORCEMENT

Since the 1986 Immigration Reform and Control Act, the biggest missing piece in the enforcement effort has been the absence of any serious attempt to discourage employers from hiring undocumented workers. The grand bargain of 1986 was supposed to offer legalization for those already here in exchange for much tougher enforcement measures to bar the employment of illegal workers in the future. In practice, for both political and technological reasons, the employer sanctions provisions have not been adequately enforced, particularly not in recent years. Many employers were simply unable to determine the legal status of some workers, and others were not much interested in trying. Further, employers who knowingly violated the rules were rarely fined, and when they were, the fines were minimal and readily seen as a cost of doing business. At the same time, the legislation fell short of being comprehensive because it failed to offer any new legal channels for immigration or temporary work. The result was that rather than discouraging illegal immigration, the 1986 act almost certainly accelerated it. That has left the American public rightly cynical of any similar grand bargain in the future. But the egregious failure of the U.S. government to carry out what had been promised in the 1986 legislation should not be used to discredit the entire approach. The failure was not conception; it was implementation.

Employment opportunities are the magnet that pulls most illegal migrants to the United States; if those opportunities can be diminished, illegal immigration will also diminish. *The Task Force believes employer sanctions need to be strengthened to discourage employers from hiring unauthorized workers; there should be clear guidelines to enable employers to comply with employer sanctions law, and these laws should be enforced to achieve optimal deterrence. Such measures are the most effective and humane way to discourage illegal migration to the United States.* There will always be a certain degree of gray-market employment, and in sectors like agriculture and construction it will be particularly difficult to end all such hiring. But far more can be done. The government must strengthen the penalties it levies against employers who hire unauthorized migrants and make it easier for willing employers to comply with the law. In particular, the government needs to improve and expand what is still a fledgling electronic verification system, E-Verify, which will permit employers to avoid prosecution by verifying against a government database that the employee applying for a job is legally entitled to work in the United States. In addition, the agency in charge of enforcing employer sanctions—Immigration and Customs Enforcement—must have adequate resources to conduct investigations and to initiate prosecutions for employers who violate the law.

Why should enforcement at the work site be any more effective than it was after 1986? In some ways, the problem is more difficult because the hiring of unauthorized migrants is so pervasive that many employers have a strong incentive to continue the practice. On the other hand, the U.S. government now has the capability to use information technologies that allow for quicker and more accurate verification that new employees are authorized to work in the United States. The E-Verify system, begun on a pilot basis in 1997, has gradually been expanded to encompass many more employers. The system permits employers to check the work eligibility of new hires online by verifying the information they provide against Social Security Administration and USCIS databases. So far, more than 100,000 companies have signed up, some states are pressuring employers to participate by doing state business only with companies that use the system, and some like Arizona require its use by most employers. Overall, about one in eight new hires in the United States is now being checked through the E-Verify system.

Although still in its infancy, the E-Verify system shows considerable promise. According to the Government Accountability Office, the vast majority of E-Verify queries (about 92 percent) are resolved instantly, and DHS claims an accuracy rate of more than 96 percent. The remainder cannot be resolved immediately because of mismatches in the Social Security database, and about 1 percent of cases involve discrepancies with USCIS data. These are not inconsequential numbers, and they force many individuals to deal with the Social Security bureaucracy to try to ensure that the database contains current and accurate information. If they are working lawfully, however, fixing any such errors is necessary to ensure that their wages are properly credited for retirement benefits. Also, the system is not yet effective in pinpointing individuals with stolen identification documents, though the addition of photographs to the verification system should help. But errors and false positives are issues that can be addressed through continued improvements in the system and increased manpower and resources at DHS and the Social Security Administration.[116] E-Verify is not yet ready for mandatory use by all employers, and DHS secretary Janet Napolitano was wise to delay making it compulsory for government contractors. It must be sufficiently transparent that employers and potential hires will be protected from errors inherent in any database system. But it is evident that E-Verify can be improved to the point where it could become mandatory on passage of comprehensive immigration reform legislation, functioning for the first time in U.S. history as a reasonably accurate system for verifying eligibility for employment.

The most controversial aspect of the recent enforcement campaigns has been the raids by ICE officials on companies suspected of employing large numbers of unauthorized immigrants. Such raids do not constitute a large portion of U.S. enforcement. Less than 2 percent of ICE's 2009 budget, for instance, is dedicated to workplace enforcement, and the number of arrests at workplaces remains significantly smaller than it was in the 1990s. But the raids have been highly controversial, in part because of their disproportionate impact on workers, which has included criminal prosecution in hundreds of cases, and the relatively modest number of employers who have been punished. Although it is perfectly reasonable to put illegal migrants caught in such raids into removal proceedings, the reason for the raids is primarily to send a strong message to companies that flout the law by hiring these workers. The highly publicized 2008 raid on a meatpacking plant in Postville, Iowa, for example, shut down a business that was rife with both immigration and labor violations, including child labor, physical abuse, hazardous working conditions, and wages that were below the legal minimum. Tough action against such companies, including criminal charges against management where warranted, is critical to sending a message to other employers who build businesses that depend on the use of low-paid and ill-treated illegal migrant workers.

Generally, employer sanctions have been almost an afterthought in the U.S. enforcement regime, even as all other aspects of enforcement have been ramped up significantly in recent years. From 2003 to 2008, the number of administrative arrests of employers for violations increased substantially, from 445 to more than 5,000. But even that was less than the level of the late 1990s.[117] More egregiously, between 2003 and 2008, only eighty-five employers were fined for hiring violations, versus five hundred to one thousand per year in the mid-1990s.

The limited enforcement of employer sanctions can be explained by the ubiquity of the violations, lack of resources, the rampant use of fraudulent documents, the lack of clarity in government guidelines, and the weakness of the sanctions for those who get caught. Much like traffic cops who have taken to ticketing only dangerous drivers rather than all speeders, routine and widespread violation of the law makes enforcement extremely difficult and challenging. It will take strengthened employer sanctions, along with a robust electronic verification system that provides immunity from prosecution for employers who use it, to achieve compliance by the vast majority of U.S. employers. This, in turn, would permit focused and targeted investigations and prosecution of noncompliant employers, further increasing the deterrent effect of the strengthened law. There is a tipping point where violations become the exception, but getting to it will require tougher sanctions. Both the carrot and the stick are needed.

The Task Force believes that as more legal immigrant workers become available, and as the government increasingly puts in place tools to encourage and to make it easier for legitimate companies to comply with the law, tough enforcement against violations by employers needs to become routine.

BORDER ENFORCEMENT

The United States has made impressive strides in the past several years in strengthening its border enforcement measures. Border enforcement is vital to safeguarding the nation against those who would do it harm, particularly terrorists and serious criminals, and for keeping out those trying to enter the United States illegally. Along with a comprehensive reform of the immigration system that allows new legal paths for immigrants, border enforcement is needed for deterring and catching those who would still try to enter the United States illegally. As the experience of the 1986 legislation has shown, there cannot be meaningful and lasting reform of U.S. legal immigration policies without an effective system to secure the borders.

The fundamental goal of border enforcement is to permit the United States to know, to the fullest extent possible, who is entering the country, but to do so in a way that does not disrupt legitimate cross-border movement. Border enforcement is necessary for national security reasons, but is also a central part of reestablishing the rule of law in the American immigration system. Under U.S. law, foreign citizens, as well as Americans who travel abroad, are supposed to enter the United States only through lawful ports of entry; if the United States cannot enforce that rule, it will surely continue to be violated.

Although most public attention is focused on those attempting to cross illegally between ports of entry, the biggest security challenge has been at legal ports of entry. All nineteen of the terrorists who carried out the 9/11 attacks entered the country initially on valid visas and came through lawful ports of entry. That they were overlooked was not particularly surprising. In the year before the attacks, there were more than five hundred million inspections of individuals crossing U.S. land borders or arriving at its airports (many individuals, especially at the land borders, go through inspection multiple times each year). In addition, linkages in databases among the relevant agencies to allow for tracking such a large volume of entries were sorely lacking. Even with the decline in cross-border travel since 9/11, with total border inspections down by more than 20 percent from their pre-9/11 peaks, nearly four hundred million inspections were carried out in 2008.[118]

Since 9/11, the U.S. government has launched a concerted effort to try to ensure that future terrorists can be identified and stopped on or before reaching U.S. borders, but with the least possible interference with legitimate travel. Four of the new initiatives are highlighted here:

- The US-VISIT system, which requires that all travelers to the United States, with the exception of most Mexicans and Canadian temporary visitors crossing the land borders, be fingerprinted and photographed on their arrival at the entry port. The scheme, launched in 2004, has been instrumental in preventing passport fraud, making it extremely difficult to enter the United States without a proper identity document. It has helped in identifying and apprehending serious criminals trying to enter the country. US-VISIT also has the potential to deter illegal migration by those who enter the United States on valid visas but then overstay those visas. By some estimates, as many as 40 percent of illegal immigrants in the United

States initially arrived on valid visas, though that figure is likely too high. Although logistical obstacles are significant, the United States is in the early stages of trying to develop an exit system that could help in identifying those who overstay their visas. The most likely application here would be to identify someone who previously overstayed a visa if and when he or she tried to enter the United States again in the future, though it is also possible that ICE could be informed more routinely of violations when individuals fail to "check out" of the country. To date, the US-VISIT system has been implemented with minimal disruption to legitimate travel, though efforts to create an exit system at the land borders would likely be far more problematic, and may require much more investment in personnel and infrastructure than would be reasonable, given the limited benefits. Currently, about 98 percent of land-border admissions take place outside US-VISIT.

– The United States now requires advanced passenger information on all airline passengers coming into the country, and has recently launched an Electronic System for Travel Authorization that requires overseas passengers from visa-waiver countries to be scrutinized by DHS before they even board flights for the United States. Advance passenger information allows checks against U.S. terrorist watch lists, and can help in identifying those who might pose a threat to U.S. security. Such advance information has been an extremely important addition to U.S. security. Travelers also benefit from knowing in advance of departure whether there is a problem with traveling to the United States, though redress in such cases remains problematic. The Western Hemisphere Travel Initiative (WHTI) requires the use of passports or other secure documents for all travelers within the hemisphere, including Americans traveling abroad and Canadians crossing the northern land border. The full rollout had been delayed over reasonable concerns that those living in the border regions did not yet fully understand the new document requirements, or might be unwilling to go to the expense of acquiring a passport. Several states, including Washington, Michigan, and New York, are issuing new, secure driver's licenses that will be accepted as border crossing documents in lieu of a passport, and the State Department in 2008 introduced a cheaper passport card for travel to Canada, Mexico, and the Caribbean, though it can only be used for land and sea entries and not for international air travel. The document requirements of WHTI were fully implemented on June 1, 2009. Although there are legitimate concerns over the impact on cross-border travel, which has declined at many Canadian border entry points since 9/11, secure documentation is essential to border security, and the WHTI should help to close a significant vulnerability.

– The expansion of trusted traveler programs such as NEXUS and SENTRI to vet and preclear travelers and to provide expedited border processing, including Easy Pass lanes. More than 200,000 U.S., Canadian, and Mexican citizens who cross borders frequently are enrolled in these trusted traveler programs, and enrollment has been growing rapidly in the past several years. It is important, however, that standards for NEXUS and SENTRI be applied in a balanced manner to address possible security threats posed by applicants but not disqualify those who pose no danger.

The Task Force endorses these and other smart border measures designed to help keep terrorists and criminals out of the country with the least possible disruption to legitimate cross-border travel, which is the core mission of the Department of Homeland Security. As they are developed and refined, these systems could also discourage illegal immigration through ports of entry by improving the ability of the United States to identify people who have previously violated the terms of their admission to the United States. But ports of entry are still likely to remain a major vulnerability simply because of the volume of inspections that must be conducted, the limited capacity at too many of the ports, and the lack of available staff.

Border enforcement between ports of entry poses an even greater logistical challenge, simply because of the scale of the terrain that must be monitored. At both the northern and southern borders, the United States must recognize that border enforcement cannot be entirely a unilateral undertaking. American initiatives need to be supplemented by close cooperation with Canadian and Mexican authorities. Canada and the United States, for instance, worked together to pioneer many of the smart border measures that have been rolled out since 9/11.[119] Although there have been points of friction, the two governments share a strong interest in cooperating to keep out terrorists who pose a serious threat to both countries. Mexico too has worked very closely with the United

States on counterterrorism-related initiatives. As mentioned earlier, there is a deep recognition at the highest levels of the Mexican government that, were a terrorist attack to be carried out in the United States by individuals who had crossed the border from Mexico, the result would be a clampdown on the border that would severely damage Mexican economic interests. In terms of discouraging illegal immigration across the southern border, however, the United States still needs to rely primarily on its own domestic means. In addition to government-to-government cooperation, there needs to be closer, ongoing cooperation between U.S. government officials responsible for securing the border and the local border communities that are most directly affected by enforcement policies.

The Task Force believes that enforcement between legal ports of entry has three central components: first, the United States needs the ability to detect illegal border crossings; second, it needs enough manpower to apprehend a high percentage of those detected; and, third, there must be serious consequences for those caught repeatedly crossing the border illegally.

The creation of a virtual border under what was known as the Secure Border Initiative, launched in 2005, is the single most ambitious undertaking DHS is currently carrying out. When fully implemented, what is now known as SBInet has the potential to enhance U.S. border capabilities in two important respects. First, it will help target U.S. Border Patrol efforts. Even with the large number of border agents currently deployed, it is not possible to have a physical law enforcement presence along the entire 2,000-mile border with Mexico. Detection technologies are a force multiplier. By deploying a network of cameras and sensors that help identify unauthorized border crossings, the Border Patrol will be better armed to respond where and when necessary, rather than simply fanning out along the border in the hopes of deterring or apprehending border crossers.

Second, even where the Border Patrol remains unable to apprehend some border crossers, detection technology will for the first time give the United States a clearer sense of who and what is being missed. Estimates of the number of illegal border crossers remain exactly that— estimates based on extrapolations from the number of people being caught. Customs and Border Protection officials believe that about two-thirds of those who try to cross illegally are caught, but that is only an educated guess. One in every three times, a determined individual is likely to get through successfully. The denominator—the total number of people attempting to cross—is unknown. By deploying detection technologies that give the United States full visibility over its southern border, from cameras to sensors to aerial vehicles, the government will for the first time be able to get an accurate reading on the scale of the problem. Such information is critical to ultimately stemming the flow of illegal migrants, and will pay benefits in other areas such as curbing drug smuggling and controlling violence in the border region.

Finally, the United States needs to consider measures that will discourage unauthorized migrants from making multiple attempts to cross the border. Currently, most Mexicans apprehended near the southern border are simply sent back to Mexico and left to try again, though the Department of Justice in December 2005 instituted programs aimed at prosecuting even some first-time illegal entry offenders with criminal misdemeanor charges. Non-Mexicans, by contrast, are faced with a formal deportation process to return them to their home countries, which can bar them from legally returning to the United States. Higher penalties for repeated illegal border crossers—including prosecution in the United States—would have a more powerful deterrent effect than the current regime, particularly if those individuals are made aware of the potential legal consequences of multiple attempts. But these penalties would need to be implemented in a more targeted fashion than some of the current efforts, which have resulted in misdemeanor charges against first-time offenders clogging up the federal courts in border states.[120]

COOPERATION WITH STATE AND LOCAL GOVERNMENTS

One of the most significant initiatives in recent years is the expanded role of state and local police forces in immigration-related enforcement. Police have long had powers to investigate and make arrests for criminal violations of immigration laws, such as human smuggling or illegal reentry into the United States by individuals barred from the country. But routine immigration law violations have long been treated as civil, not criminal offenses, and have traditionally been handled by federal immigration authorities. In 1996, the Illegal Immigration Reform and Immigrant Responsibility Act created a formal mechanism for federal agencies to enter into agreements with state and local police to enforce civil immigration laws. The primary purpose was to make certain that illegal immigrants who commit serious crimes are identified and removed from the country. Under these agreements, designated officers are trained in immigration enforcement and then perform certain specified immigration-related duties. These officers are usually limited to specific investigative forces, such as narcotics or homicide, and those responsible for checking the immigration status of new arrests when they are jailed. But in other cases the powers have been more broadly delegated. The first agreement under this provision, known as 287(g), was signed with the state of Florida in 2002. Currently nearly seventy state and local police departments have entered into 287(g) agreements.

There is no question that involving local police forces in immigration enforcement is a huge force multiplier. Immigration and Customs Enforcement has just over 5,500 criminal investigators; in comparison, there are more than 675,000 police officers and more than 700,000 prison officials working across the country. The likelihood of identifying illegal immigrants—particularly those who have committed crimes and are thus the greatest cause for concern—increases dramatically if these state and local officials are empowered to check an individual's immigration status. The reluctance of many jurisdictions to carry out such checks is a significant limitation on the ability of the federal government to identify and remove illegal immigrants living in the United States.

But there are also good reasons for such reluctance. State and local police forces are responsible for a broad range of law enforcement activities, which requires interaction and close cooperation with the communities they police. Their primary missions are to prevent crimes in their communities, to come to the assistance of crime victims, and to arrest or sanction those who commit crimes, regardless of their immigration status. Criminals often target illegal migrants as their victims, and strict enforcement of immigration laws may interfere with effective prosecution of more serious crimes. Immigration enforcement may put local officials in an extremely difficult situation because of the need to build close ties with a community that includes a significant population of illegal migrants. If those individuals are too frightened to interact with police, the effectiveness of those police forces will suffer. Immigration enforcement may also pull scarce resources away from other core law-enforcement missions. Finally, because of the preponderance of Mexicans, Central Americans, and other Hispanics in the undocumented population, it is far too easy for the local enforcement of immigration laws to slip into racial profiling that can violate the civil rights of legal American residents and citizens. Because of these concerns, some local police forces have refused to cooperate with federal immigration authorities on the full range of immigration enforcement.

The current situation with regard to cooperation between federal and local law enforcement is far from satisfactory. Some of the country's large cities, where such cooperation could be most beneficial, have put restrictions in place on the ability of state and local police forces to check or report on an individual's immigration status. In other cases, some local law enforcement agencies have interpreted their role broadly and begun checking the immigration status of individuals after routine traffic violation stops or other minor offenses. The danger is actions that are tantamount to police sweeps to identify immigration violators, which is far beyond what Congress envisioned when the 287(g) provision was enacted. One study in a Tennessee county, for instance, found that the arrest rate for Hispanics driving without a license doubled after the enactment of a 287(g) agreement, indicating that more Hispanic drivers were being targeted only to check their immigration status. In North Carolina, the overwhelming number of apprehensions made under 287(g) is for routine traffic violations.[121]

The primary reason that state and local enforcement of immigration laws are so controversial is that the immigration system has been broken for so long that millions live in the United States illegally, and there is little agreement, beyond that about deporting serious criminals, on how aggressive the country should be in identifying and removing such individuals. Comprehensive immigration reform legislation and a dramatically smaller illegal population would make it much easier for federal and local authorities to cooperate in upholding immigration laws.

REDRESS PROCEDURES

As the government continues to expand its use of information technologies in an effort to identify who is authorized to be in the United States and who is not, the issue of false positives has become more acute. Any effort to keep better track of such vast numbers of people is inevitably going to result in mistakes, and because of the large numbers even a very small error rate can have very large consequences. The terrorist watch list, for example, though it has proven its worth as a law enforcement tool, grew at such a rapid pace after 9/11 that many people found themselves improperly on the list. Between 2004 and 2008, the number of names on the terrorist watch list grew from 160,000 to more than 850,000, and has recently exceeded one million names (though this number includes multiple spellings of some names). The process continues to lack the kind of careful vetting that should precede the decisions to list individuals. Yet only within the past year has the government finally set up an easily accessible redress procedure, though its effectiveness remains to be demonstrated.

As E-Verify grows, it is becoming another area in which effective and speedy redress provisions are extremely important. Individuals who believe they have been wrongly identified by the system must have a quick, efficient, and accurate way to clarify and resolve their status. No one should be denied a job because they are improperly believed to be living illegally in the United States.

EARNED LEGALIZATION

The toughest issue is what to do with the millions already living illegally in the United States. This, more than any other issue, led to the failure of congressional efforts at immigration reform in 2006 and 2007. By the best estimates, slightly fewer than twelve million unauthorized immigrants are thought to be living currently in the United States, though that number is likely shrinking as a result of the weakening economy and tougher enforcement.[122] Public opinion polls, perhaps surprisingly, show that about two-thirds of Americans support finding a way for those who live illegally in the United States to gain lawful status, providing they develop English-language skills, pass background checks, and pay some sort of restitution. But deep suspicion rightly remains that a mass legalization will simply repeat the 1986 experience and do nothing to stem the problem of illegal migration in the future.

Language matters a great deal in the debate over immigration, but it matters here particularly. The legalization provisions in many of the bills considered by Congress from 2004 to 2007 were denounced by some critics as amnesty. More than any other single argument, it was the amnesty claim that did the most to kill the legislation. By any reasonable definition, however, the use of the term *amnesty* to describe the proposed reforms was a gross misstatement. The *Merriam-Webster*

Dictionary defines amnesty as the "the act of an authority (as a government) by which pardon is granted to a large group of individuals." In other words, amnesty means wiping a transgressor's record clean—it is a free ride.[123] Moreover, amnesty implies a serious threat of criminal prosecution and conviction. Like it or not, for the millions of illegal immigrants in the United States, there has never been a serious threat of criminal prosecution. When President Jimmy Carter offered amnesty to those who had evaded the draft for the Vietnam War, they were simply forgiven and welcomed home. There was a real threat of prosecution for draft evasion, and the pardon assured that they could not be prosecuted or be required to perform additional public service, pay fines, or otherwise make amends.

Consider, in contrast, the provisions in the various immigration reform bills before Congress during the Bush administration. Even the most generous bills would have required those living in the United States unlawfully to earn their legalization. Illegal migrants would have had to demonstrate a long, virtually uninterrupted period of gainful employment, pass criminal and national security background checks, pay substantial fines, and demonstrate basic mastery of English. In a number of versions of the legislation, those who qualified would only be eligible initially for a temporary work visa, and would need to live and work in the United States for another significant period before being permitted to seek permanent residence.

Other, more targeted bills such as the Development, Relief, and Education for Alien Minors (DREAM) Act were aimed at providing some path to legalization for children who were brought to the United States illegally by their parents and thus had no active part in the decision to violate U.S. immigration laws. Those who had been present in the United States for at least five years, had earned a high school diploma, had been admitted to a postsecondary program, and had demonstrated good moral character would be eligible to adjust to permanent residence. The Agricultural Job Opportunities, Benefits, and Security (AgJOBS) Act would similarly have offered temporary status to those already employed as farm workers. If they remained in good standing for the following three to six years, those individuals could seek permanent residence.

In each of these proposals, the starting point was not whether the United States would wipe the record clean and treat illegal migrants as

though they arrived here legally, but whether the country should provide a path to allow them to earn the right to remain in the United States.
Americans are rightly dismissive of amnesty, but there is a much more
compelling argument for earned legalization, for allowing individuals
through their actions to demonstrate that they are willing to make sacrifices for the privilege of full membership in American society.

The strongest argument against some form of earned legalization
is that it will simply set the United States up for further illegal immigration and another round of legalization one or two or three decades
from now. The experience of 1986 serves as a stark warning, and there
is indeed a degree of moral hazard in any legalization scheme. There is
no question that earned legalization creates an incentive for others to
try to enter the United States illegally in the hope that they too will be
allowed to stay by a future act of legalization. *The Task Force believes it is
critical that any legalization program be accompanied both by more realistic
immigration and temporary worker quotas and by stringent enforcement.*

Weighed against those arguments are the stronger, practical, ethical, economic, and national security arguments in favor of earned
legalization. Practically, the difficulties in deporting so many illegal
immigrants are extraordinary. Although not impossible, by any measure the undertaking would be extremely costly. For all the resources
already been dedicated to increasing the number of removals, and
the weak economy that has encouraged some to leave on their own,
there appears to have been only a small decline in the number of illegal
migrants living in the United States. Given both the expense and the
further damage mass deportation would do to America's economy and
to its reputation as a nation of immigrants, such an effort would not be
in the country's interest.

The United States has long been a country that believes in second
chances. The alternative—to break up families and wrench people away
from communities where they have lived for many years, and in some
cases even decades—is morally unacceptable. In many cases, it would
require breaking up families in which some of the members are undocumented, others are legal residents, and others, particularly children,
were born in the United States and are therefore U.S. citizens. These
dilemmas are apparent even in the current enforcement effort. As a
result of the new document requirements under the Western Hemisphere Travel Initiative, for example, many Americans who have lived

their entire lives near the southern border with Mexico are applying for passports for the first time. But a significant number have seen the validity of their birth certificates questioned because some midwives in the region had a history of fraudulently registering babies who were actually born across the border in Mexico as Americans. Some of those whose identities have been called into question include current U.S. Customs and Border Protection officials as well as members of the U.S. military. Although suspicions about the validity of some birth certificates may indeed be legitimate, is the United States really going to deport these people?[124] This small example shows the difficulties of any approach that posits removing most illegal migrants from the United States.

Economically, the existence of a kind of shadow workforce that comprises more than 5 percent of the U.S. workforce makes little sense.[125] Given the danger of deportation, it is impossible for these workers to press for better wages or working conditions. The result is an unfair advantage to employers who hire undocumented immigrants rather than native-born workers or legal migrants. Normalizing the status of undocumented workers in the United States could help improve both wages and working conditions for all those in lower-skilled jobs, and create fairer competition for American workers.[126]

Finally, the security dangers of allowing a large, unauthorized population to remain are substantial. Effective homeland security requires that the U.S. government know who is living in this country to the greatest extent possible. It is simply not safe to allow so many to live a shadow existence in the country. Efforts at deportation will only drive such people further underground in an effort to evade immigration enforcement, when U.S. security would be better served by making their presence here lawful.

As unsatisfactory as it is to many from a rule-of-law perspective, including members of this Task Force, we believe there is little choice but to find some way to bring illegal migrants already in the United States who wish to remain out of the shadows and to offer them an earned pathway to legal status. It is the right policy choice—for economic reasons, for security reasons, and for the simply pragmatic reason that the United States should not attempt to deport people who have lived here for a long time, raised their families here, worked hard, and otherwise obeyed the law.

IMMIGRANT INTEGRATION

Although there has been a great deal of national debate over illegal immigration, there has been essentially none about how to respond to the millions of new legal immigrants once they are here and the millions more who will arrive in the years ahead, whatever happens to illegal immigration. Rapid immigration is traumatic, both for the immigrants and for the receiving communities. This is especially true in regards to new immigrant destinations away from the traditional entry points in major coastal cities. Those smaller cities and towns, especially in the South, the Midwest, and the Rocky Mountain states, are now receiving a disproportionate share of the latest wave of immigrants, an experience mostly without precedent in their histories.

The United States is unique among the major Western powers in having no national policy on immigrant integration, despite the massive numbers of immigrants (legal and illegal). In the past, many of these integration functions were performed by a variety of local and national groups and institutions, from political parties to church and community groups to a military in which most young men served. But these integrating institutions have weakened over time, and no alternatives have emerged to take their place. Three examples follow:

– *English-language education.* Lost in the political furor over English-only policies that some states have adopted and others have considered is that all sides in the immigration debate, including immigrants, recognize the importance of learning to speak America's national language. Much research shows that the ability to speak English is central to successfully adapting to American society, and is the primary determinant of whether new immigrants increase their earning power. Yet there is little government support (and virtually no federal support) for English-language classes, so the relatively few programs that are available have long waiting lists. Virtually every other major Western country provides generous government support for language training, the costs of which are small relative to the long-run economic, social, and civic benefits. Just as the United States supports universal public education because it believes the results benefit the whole community, so too should it provide much more public support for English classes for new immigrants, because the results will flow to the whole community.

– *Federal support for local areas affected by recent, rapid immigration.* Most careful studies show that the primary fiscal benefits from immigration (in terms of economic productivity and contributions to the Social Security system) accrue at the national level, whereas the primary fiscal costs (especially for educational and medical services) fall on states and localities. This situation justifies federal aid to affected local areas. For example, in the years during and after World War II, when a massive nationwide system of military bases was necessary for national defense, the federal government provided impact grants to affected local school systems. This same logic should apply to other support services and advice to local governments in areas without immigration experience. For instance, the British government, with support from both major parties, provides substantial financial and advisory assistance to areas most affected by recent immigration.

– *Civic education.* The last time the United States faced—and ultimately managed successfully—a massive wave of immigration was between 1890 and 1914. During that period, American schools were recognized as critical to the assimilation process, in terms of both positioning the children of immigrants for successful adaptation to America and creating a more encompassing sense of national identity. Many curricular reforms were introduced to accomplish those goals. Similarly, in most other major Western nations today, education is recognized as a critical tool for fostering the integration of immigrants, both civically and economically. In the United States today, by contrast, education for a massive new generation of U.S. citizens has been recognized as a priority in neither the national debate about education nor in the national debate about immigration.

None of this is to say that new immigrants need to give up their ethnic identities to become full members of American society. The history of American immigration and the prominence of hyphenated identities (Italian-American, Irish-American, African-American, and so on) demonstrate that one can be a good American yet retain a strong sense of ethnic identity. One of the secrets to America's success as an immigrant society is the historic commitment to such diversity. The same cannot be said for many European countries that face greater struggles in dealing with their new immigrants.

Policies aimed at successful immigrant integration across the country are not just important in and of themselves. They are also relevant to generating a political climate more conducive to reasoned examination of the other national and international issues related to immigration. If American communities were helped in dealing with the unfamiliar challenges posed by immigration at the grass roots, then Americans might feel more comfortable addressing the larger national and international issues less emotionally and more rationally.

There are some encouraging signs that the federal government is prepared to tackle this problem more directly. The administration's Task Force on New Americans, for instance, created by President George W. Bush in 2006, has focused attention on the need for what it called "a concerted national effort to ensure the successful integration of our current wave of immigrants."[127] Congress has considered legislation that would provide $200 million to $300 million annually for new English-language and civics training for adults and would support other integration-related activities.

Given the general lack of government support, however, what is telling is not that the current generation of immigrants is failing to integrate, but that they appear to be doing so well regardless. Detailed studies on English-language acquisition by immigrants, for instance, have shown that English-language use increases considerably even among first-generation immigrants the longer they remain in the United States. In addition, the U.S-born children of Spanish-speaking immigrants quickly become more fluent in English than in Spanish, a pattern that holds even for foreign-born children who are brought here at a young age.[128]

The Task Force finds that U.S. interests are best served when immigrants are integrated into American society, and particularly when they acquire the English-language skills that are a prerequisite to success in most occupations and to full participation in civic life. This objective is perfectly consistent with immigrants maintaining vibrant ethnic identities, just as millions of the descendants of previous waves of immigrants—from Irish-Americans to Japanese-Americans—do today. The federal government should develop a national policy on immigrant integration that focuses in particular on helping state and local institutions provide English-language training, civic education, and other forms of support.

Recommendations

Getting immigration policy right is vital to America's national interests—to its economic prosperity, to its national security, and to its standing in the world. The continued drift and failure to reform U.S. institutions for handling immigration and U.S. borders has already been very costly, and will become even more so the longer this situation persists. Yet political divisions have made it difficult to move forward with necessary changes, and the current economic recession has made the task no easier. The CFR-sponsored Independent Task Force, a bipartisan group, has come together around an analysis and a set of recommendations we believe offer the broad outlines of a way out of this impasse. Legislation—comprehensive immigration reform—is needed to address the enormous array of challenges, as is a range of administrative and procedural improvements. Despite the difficulty of the challenges, the United States has the understanding, the capabilities, and the incentives to move forward and create a more intelligent, better functioning immigration system that will serve the country's interests. It is time to get on with the job.

COMPREHENSIVE IMMIGRATION REFORM

The United States needs a fundamental overhaul of its immigration laws. The Task Force believes the Obama administration and Congress must prepare the political ground and work to pass legislation at the earliest possible date, and is encouraged by moves in that direction. Overhauling dysfunctional immigration laws and providing new, efficient channels for legal immigration would help to foster economic recovery, and will make the United States a stronger country as it climbs out of the recession. In addition, the large population of illegal immigrants remains a serious problem that degrades the rule of law, increases security risks, and creates unfair competition for native-born workers. The effort to reform immigration laws, however, should not be used as an excuse for failing to make progress on a host of specific problems in the immigration system that must be addressed regardless of legislative changes, and that could serve to enhance the effectiveness of legislative reform. *The Task Force recommends that a new effort to pass a comprehensive immigration reform bill be a first-tier priority for the Obama administration and Congress, and should be restarted without delay.*

Any immigration reform effort should include nine major elements: attracting skilled immigrants, limited temporary worker programs, family-based immigration, a streamlined and flexible system, government investment, earned legalization, employment enforcement, border enforcement, and state and local enforcement.

ATTRACTING SKILLED IMMIGRANTS

The United States needs to develop a conscious and explicit policy for attracting highly skilled immigrants. For most of its history, America has enjoyed a considerable skills and education advantage over its largest economic competitors. This is unfortunately no longer the case. Other countries are producing highly skilled workers faster than the United States, and such individuals will be in increasingly high demand in the U.S. economy in the coming years.[129] America's economic future, as well as its diplomatic success, depends greatly on its ability to attract a significant share of the best and brightest immigrants from around the world. *The Task Force recommends that the United States tackle head-on the growing competition for skilled immigrants from other countries and make the goal of attracting such immigrants a central component of its immigration policy. For decades, the primary goal has been to ration admission; in the future, recruiting the immigrants it wants must be the highest priority.*

America's universities represent the biggest competitive advantage the United States enjoys in attracting talented immigrants. Rather than handcuffing its universities, the United States should be exploiting that advantage. Of the roughly 600,000 foreign students in the United States, more than half attend just 150 universities and colleges, and account for just 3 percent of enrollment in higher education. These numbers could easily be expanded without displacing American students. Although American universities remain a magnet for talent from all over the world, government policies do too little to help them.

In particular, the United States makes it exceedingly difficult for foreign students to remain in the country to work after graduation, though many find ways to do so regardless. Roughly half the foreign students who acquire green cards do so by marriage to American citizens or permanent residents; another 10 percent are related to American citizens or permanent residents and acquire green cards through family preferences.[130] The decision by Congress in 2005 to add another 20,000 H-1B visas for foreign students who receive graduate degrees from American universities has helped, but still excludes many thousands of top-level graduates who might otherwise choose to remain in the United States.

The Task Force recommends that foreign students who earn graduate degrees from American universities should be presumptively eligible to seek work in the United States and to receive employment-based visas. The exceptions would be students who come on scholarship programs (such as the U.S. Fulbright scholarship) that require them to return home after their program of study, unless waived for just cause. There should be no quotas on the number of foreign students eligible for work visas.

There are other ways in which the United States could make itself more attractive to skilled workers. For these individuals, the temporary visa system has become the route to permanent residence and eventually citizenship in the United States. More than 90 percent of the green cards given to high-skilled immigrants are awarded to those already working here on temporary visas. There are two fundamental problems: first, under most economic conditions, the quotas on the number of temporary work visas for skilled workers are not flexible enough to meet demand; second, the number of employment-based green cards is, under most economic conditions, too low to allow skilled workers to make the transition to permanent residence. *The Task Force recommends that quotas for skilled work visas like the H-1B visa be increased, but fluctuate in line with economic conditions. Similarly, the number of employment-based green cards should not face a hard cap, but should be allowed to increase and decrease as economic conditions warrant. Under most economic conditions, the number of employment-based green cards should be significantly higher than current levels.*

The United States should retain a labor market test for the handful of companies that are heavy users of H-1B visas to ensure that they are also seeking qualified American workers. The United States could even consider restricting the percentage of H-1B workers that any single company could hire. But in general, companies should be free to employ skilled foreign workers without having to jump through expensive and time-consuming hurdles to prove that they cannot find American workers. There is simply no good empirical evidence that foreign workers are depressing wages, even in the skilled fields in which they are most abundant, such as computer programming and software engineering.[131] The best way to prevent hiring abuses is for the government to fund and prioritize enforcement to ensure that H-1B workers are paid appropriately and not used to undercut similarly qualified American workers. In principle, however, it makes no sense to restrict the immigration of those skilled workers who are highly sought after by many countries, and who would bring the greatest economic benefits to the United States.

There are other problems with the current legal regime underlying the H-1B and some other categories of temporary visas. The United States has for a long time attempted to maintain a rigid division between temporary, nonimmigrant visas, and permanent immigrant visas. For many categories of short-term visas, this continues to make sense—those who come to the United States on tourist visas, business visas, or seasonal employment visas like the H-2A and H-2B are expected to return home before their visas expire. But those workers on H-1B visas or other categories of skilled-worker visas are in many cases individuals that the United States would like to see remain permanently. Yet the existing regime makes it very difficult for them to do so. Too many would-be immigrants find themselves living in the United States for long periods without being able to convert to permanent status. This has many negative ramifications. In most cases, the spouses of temporary visa holders are not permitted to work. Travel outside the United States becomes more difficult and expensive. Fees must be paid regularly to maintain status. Changing jobs is also difficult because individuals may fear losing their visa status within the United States.

This situation argues for two changes. First, with regard to visas that permit individuals to work in the United States, the government should do away with some of the restrictions that apply to those on a genuinely temporary basis, such as tourist, student, or business visas. *For those in the United States on temporary work visas, with the exception of seasonal work visas like the H-2A and the H-2B, the Task Force recommends eliminating the current requirement that these visa holders demonstrate the intent to not immigrate to the United States. Such a requirement is an anachronism that does not reflect how immigration to the United States actually takes place for most people, and does not recognize the U.S.*

national interest in encouraging some of those visa holders to remain in the United States permanently. Enforcing this rule also diverts scarce consular and border inspection resources away from other, more pressing responsibilities. Such a change would obviously not apply to the many individuals who come to the United States on visitor, business, student, or other nonimmigrant visas, and would still have to demonstrate their intention not to immigrate as part of their admission.

Another problem is the limitations posed by nationality quotas on green cards. In an effort to promote a more diverse immigrant population, the United States sets quotas on the number of individuals who can receive green cards each year, with the length of the wait determined by the nationality of the applicant and the category under which he or she seeks to become a permanent immigrant. Although diversity in immigration is a laudable goal, restricting permanent immigration by highly skilled workers on this basis is not in America's interest. In particular, it artificially restricts immigrants from India and China whom many U.S. companies are eager to attract. *The Task Force therefore recommends eliminating the nationality quotas for skilled workers.*

The Task Force considered, but did not endorse, creating a points system that would mirror those in Canada, Australia, and the United Kingdom, as Congress briefly considered in 2007. Although such schemes have many merits, they have one significant drawback: they set the government up as the primary arbiter of what skills are deemed critical for the economy. Given the limitations of economic forecasting tools, such schemes often end up setting inappropriate criteria for admission. The United States has generally had more success by giving visas to those who have job offers from American companies, thus leaving the private sector to make the determinations about what skills are most needed for its businesses.

TEMPORARY WORKER PROGRAMS

Although the U.S. economy has exhibited an enormous and continued appetite for low-skilled labor, the immigration system simply does not recognize the demand. The quotas for employment-based admission by low-skilled immigrants are miniscule, and in practice most of the demand is filled by unauthorized immigrants. Recognizing that the U.S. economy has had and will continue to have a significant appetite for low-skilled workers is a critical part of gaining control over illegal immigration. One of the most significant failings of the 1986 IRCA was that it failed to make any new provisions for future immigration—either temporary or permanent—for lower-skilled workers. Yet the widespread availability of jobs in the United States for such workers proved an irresistible magnet. This will continue to be true when economic recovery takes hold, and demand will grow over time as the American population continues to age. A central part of any immigration reform package must be a series of measures for lower-skilled workers.

There are three broad possibilities for addressing immigration by low-skilled workers: continued tight restrictions, a large temporary worker program, or increased quotas for visas that could lead to permanent residence coupled with a smaller temporary worker program.

Continuing tight restrictions—the status quo—has on its face been a failure. To date, it has served only to encourage high numbers of unskilled immigrants to come to the United States illegally. Even if enforcement alone could dry up that flow, which the Task Force does not believe is feasible, the U.S. economy would suffer, because of both the high cost of enforcement measures and the resulting losses to the economy that would result from trying to divert better-educated native-born workers into lower-skilled employment.

A large temporary worker program has greater appeal, but the experience in Europe and in other places should be cautionary. The difficulty with such programs is that unless they allow some avenue for permanent residence, many temporary workers are likely to remain permanently in violation of the law. Some European countries now have large, disaffected populations of so-called temporary workers who have no possibility of ever acquiring citizenship. Europe is facing a problem with disaffected, radicalized Muslim youth that so far the United States has been spared, and the difference in the handling of immigration policy is a significant reason. The American practice of expecting that immigrants will embrace American values and become full members of American society through citizenship has been far more successful.

The largest studies of U.S. immigration policy—including the Select Commission on Immigration and Refugee Policy in the late 1970s (the Hesburgh Commission) and the U.S. Commission on Immigration Reform in the 1990s (the Jordan Commission)—have argued against large temporary worker schemes.

But even with their limitations, there is a place for temporary worker programs. In particular, such programs should make it easy for those who wish to come to the United States for seasonal or other temporary work. It is particularly important for restoring some of the historical circularity with Mexico, in which Mexicans came to the United States for work and then returned home to their families. Agriculture is the most obvious industry for such workers, but the hotel, restaurant, and tourist industries, some parts of the construction industry, and other sectors have sharp fluctuations in demand that could be met through temporary worker programs.

The Task Force recommends a two-pronged approach. First, the United States should recognize that, subject to economic fluctuations, continued demand for low-skilled labor is likely to be an ongoing feature of the economy. Therefore, the United States should allow greater numbers of low-skilled immigrants to enter on work visas, with the option of seeking permanent residence if they wish. Those numbers should be adjusted regularly based on the needs of the economy, with the goal of enhancing U.S. competitiveness. At the same time, the government should create an expanded seasonal work program—but one that is easier for employers to use and that provides better protections for the foreign workers employed in it.

Such seasonal work programs should focus primarily on offering work opportunities for residents of Mexico and Central America, the primary sources of illegal migration to the United States. The programs could be strengthened by closer cooperation with those governments designed to ensure that individuals in the program return home as their visas require. Canada, for example, has had considerable success in cooperating with Mexico and some Caribbean countries on the implementation of a seasonal agriculture worker program.

The Task Force believes that there is a place for temporary worker programs, but that they should be focused on truly temporary jobs in such industries as agriculture, hospitality, and recreation rather than used more broadly. To allow greater flexibility in the current temporary worker programs, they should be allowed to apply to jobs that may be permanent in nature but need to be filled by a temporary worker on a short-term basis. Thus, the "double temporary" requirement for qualifying positions should be eliminated. In addition, these programs should be portable, so that guest workers are not tied to a single employer and thus unable to seek better wages or working conditions, and they should be covered by all relevant wage and health and safety laws, much as any U.S.-born employee is covered. The need for additional low-skilled labor for more permanent jobs should be met instead by visa programs that allow for the possibility of permanent residence.

FAMILY-BASED IMMIGRATION

The U.S. preference for immigrants who are family members of immigrants already living in this country has a long tradition, and has demonstrated its importance in building strong immigrant communities in the United States. Family reunification accounts for about two-thirds of all permanent immigration to the United States, and is in no small measure responsible for the generally positive experience the United States has had with immigration. No immigration reform effort should undermine the central importance of family reunification.

But the system currently is not working in the interests of either immigrant families or the country as a whole. Far too many family members are left to wait years before they receive permission to immigrate to the United States. Spouses and unmarried children of permanent residents already living in the United States, for instance, can face waits of five years or more before being allowed to immigrate, a cruel and needless separation. Some 4.9 million people who have been approved for family-based visas are currently waiting until their quota numbers come up to be allowed entry to the United States.[132]

In dealing with family-based immigration, there are several choices, each of them with problems. First, the United States could leave the current system intact, but for the reasons cited, the status quo is not desirable. Indeed, the backlogs are likely to become much longer if, as the Task Force favors, there is an earned legalization program in place. As unauthorized migrants acquire permanent residence and eventually citizenship, the demand for family visas, and thus the backlog, is likely to grow even larger. That would worsen an already bad situation. Arriving here after the most productive years of their working lives have passed is in the interests of neither the immigrant families nor the country. Second, the United States could simply lift all quota restrictions on family-based immigration. That, however, would push the annual immigration numbers to levels far beyond the current record levels and remove effective control over admissions. That leaves a third choice, which is to restrict in new ways the number of family members who can be sponsored by U.S. citizens and permanent residents.

Within the Task Force, there was no clear consensus on whether it is necessary to further restrict immigration by family members outside immediate family, and if so how it should best be done. Current law allows for immigrants, as they acquire permanent residence and citizenship, to sponsor their adult children, parents, and siblings. The McCain-Kennedy comprehensive immigration reform bill that was the starting point for efforts in the last session of Congress is perhaps the most serious attempt to date to try to tackle the problem, and it is a reasonable approach. It appropriately rewarded U.S. citizens by exempting their immediate relatives—spouses, minor children, and parents—from the overall family visa quota, and then set an annual cap of 480,000 for all other family categories. It raised the country limits slightly, and then set up a preference system that favored the spouses and minor children of legal permanent residents. It had the virtue of speeding reunification of immediate families and reducing waiting times for other relatives but without significantly increasing overall numbers. Over time, such a system could gradually be adjusted to give even greater weight to immediate relatives and to reduce the number of family visas for extended families.

Another approach favored by some Task Force members would simply be to phase out the eligibility of siblings to immigrate through family sponsors, and perhaps to restrict adult children and parents as well. Others argued for the importance of extended family networks and resisted such recommendations. As in the last effort, this will be one of the most difficult issues Congress faces. The guiding principle should be to maintain the centrality of family reunification, but not expand it, and open new opportunities for legal immigration by those with needed skills but no family ties in the United States.

A STREAMLINED, FLEXIBLE SYSTEM

It is not realistic to think that the United States will ever create a simple immigration system. The number of visitors and immigrants is too large, and the need for special rules for special cases (i.e., diplomats, foreign journalists, religious workers, and so on) is such that some level of complexity will always be a feature of the system. But there is no question that the current proliferation of visa categories, with particular rules and policies attached to each, has reached a point where it works against effective administration. Reforming and simplifying immigration laws is a task as daunting as trying to simplify the Internal Revenue Code. But though efforts at simplification have been made periodically within the tax system, no similar effort has been undertaken with regard to immigration laws and regulations.

The Task Force recommends that Congress and the Obama administration establish a high-level independent commission to undertake a detailed examination of current U.S. immigration laws and regulations, and to make recommendations for simplifying the administration and improving the transparency of those rules.

One commendable model is the 2006 report of the Migration Policy Institute (MPI) task force, *Immigration and America's Future: A New Chapter*. It suggests the use of three broad categories of visas for those living and working in the United States. The temporary category would be used by short-term seasonal workers who return home each year. Provisional visas would allow U.S. companies to identify and recruit foreign workers at all skill levels. Those recruited would not be tied to a particular employer and would be eligible to seek permanent residence. Unlike the current system, the Task Force believes that this category must include a significant quota for low-skilled workers, reflecting the demand in the U.S. economy. The permanent category would mirror the current green card and be available both to those applying directly from abroad and for those here on provisional visas who wish to remain permanently.

The MPI report envisions a somewhat more radical overhaul of the current immigrant visa system than this Task Force has contemplated, but the direction it sets is the correct one. Rather than continuing to add to the already hopeless complexity of the existing system, Congress and the administration should be looking for every opportunity to make the system simpler and easier to understand and use. The legal requirements for immigrating to the United States must be simplified and applied with consistency, predictability, and transparency.

A second serious problem with the current system has been underscored by the current economic downturn. The system is relatively impervious to economic fluctuations, resulting in a shortage of immigrant workers in buoyant economic times and a surplus in recessions. Further, the United States has no ongoing institutional capacity for evaluating the need for immigrant labor, the effects of immigration on the economy, and other questions that are vital to the United States. Instead, Congress periodically adjusts the various immigration quotas, with no way of knowing whether they will be appropriate for the economic conditions of the future.

The MPI report recommended the creation of a Standing Commission on Immigration and Labor Markets, whose responsibility would be to evaluate the economic impacts of immigration, and to make recommendations regarding the appropriate size and mix of immigrant inflows. The report argues persuasively that "managing immigration in the national interest requires a[n] ... institutional capacity to monitor and analyze information as the basis for making changes."[133] The comparison with trade policy is striking. Although immigration is every bit as important as trade for the U.S. economy, the institutional expertise on immigration policy is a fraction of that in the trade world. Trade policymakers can call on a staff of several hundred economists and other experts at the independent U.S. International Trade Commission for background investigations into the effects of trade on specific industries and segments of the economy.

The proposed commission would be responsible for making recommendations to the president and Congress on levels and categories of immigration needed to support economic growth while maintaining low unemployment and preventing suppression of wages. Determining the mandate of such a commission, and its methodologies, would not be an easy task, and there is already some controversy over the possible terms of reference and the scope of its authority.[134] The Task Force believes that virtues of the U.S. immigration system—the priority given family reunification and its responsiveness to the actual needs of employers rather than to government evaluations of the labor market—must be kept intact. The MPI report calls for the commission to recommend adjustments in immigration levels every two years, but a truly flexible system would require adjustments over fairly short periods as economic conditions fluctuate. Overall levels for temporary and provisional visas in particular should be adjusted regularly. The government could consider innovative mechanisms such as an auction or another market-based system that would make immigration levels more responsive to market demand without exacerbating unemployment during recessions. Although the details need resolution, the

United States must have a more reasoned and flexible system for setting immigration levels, and an unbiased expert commission is an important part of moving in that direction.

The Task Force supports the recommendation in the MPI report that the United States establish a Standing Commission on Immigration and Labor Markets charged with making recommendations to the president on adjustments to levels and categories of immigration. The commission would carry out ongoing analyses of labor market conditions and trends, and would make recommendations for immigration levels aimed at maintaining strong economic growth and low unemployment while preventing wage suppression. Unless overridden by Congress, which would retain its existing authority to set immigration quotas, the president would adjust immigration levels periodically after receiving recommendations from the commission.

GOVERNMENT INVESTMENT

There is a critical need for refinements in how the U.S. system for processing legal visa and immigration applications is financed. Two problems in particular stand out. First, user fees are also used to pay for refugee and asylum processing, which does not generate fees on its own. Second, USCIS has enormous needs for improvements in its case management infrastructure that will involve costs beyond what the fee system can support.

Immigration is one of the most technologically demanding and complex functions of the U.S. government. Yet America's immigration services have, sadly, been among the slowest in adopting the advanced information technologies whose greatest virtue is to simplify and streamline the handling of large quantities of complex data. Ideas for such a comprehensive modernization were floated well over a decade ago, but the system remains largely paper based, resulting in long delays, lost files, and other inconveniences that can be hugely damaging for individual applicants. It has also produced a much higher rate of fraud than is acceptable. Only in the past year, for example, has it finally become possible for individuals to go online to submit applications, make appointments with immigration officers, and check the status of their cases.

U.S. Citizenship and Immigration Services has recently established a Transformation Program Office, and has put plans in place for an ambitious modernization scheme to be completed by 2013. The goal is to speed up processing times, improve security background checks, and allow easier tracking of individual applications. Yet the funding for the project remains uncertain. User fees were already raised by an average of 66 percent in 2007, and there is currently limited scope for further increases; USCIS is counting on the additional revenue from premium processing, but if the effort to reduce processing times works, the result will be a decline in those fees. *Given the larger U.S. interest in creating a better functioning legal immigration system, the Task Force recommends that Congress appropriate additional public financing for transformation.*[135]

Such transformation is particularly critical to the success of any immigration reform legislation. Under some of the scenarios envisioned, DHS would face the task of processing applications for legalization involving more than ten million new immigrants, and perhaps administering new categories of legal visas as well as an expanded temporary worker program. It is unrealistic to expect USCIS will be able to handle that additional volume of work without a larger staff and a far more robust and efficient processing system based on state-of-the-art information management technology. The success of the transformation program is critical to reforming U.S. immigration laws and should be carried out as rapidly as possible. Congress should appropriate adequate funds for carrying out this project and undertake careful oversight to ensure that it is implemented on time and on budget.

EARNED LEGALIZATION

As discussed in greater detail above, the Task Force has concluded that earned legalization is necessary and warranted for many illegal immigrants living in the United States. The current situation is dangerous for American security, corrodes respect for the rule of law, makes those immigrants vulnerable to exploitation, and creates unfair competition for American workers that erodes labor standards. But the Task Force is opposed to amnesty; instead, we favor a scheme that allows many illegal immigrants to earn the right to live in this country lawfully and to start on the path to permanent residence and citizenship.

Creating that scheme, of course, is an enormous challenge facing Congress. The conditions for legalization must be demanding enough that they bar individuals who are either a threat to this country or are unwilling to make the commitments required for full membership in American society. On the other hand, if the conditions are too onerous it may be impossible to bring many illegal migrants into the legal system.

Congress has already considered more limited legalization programs that would be an important first step in the right direction. The DREAM Act, for example, which has been reintroduced in the 111th Congress, would provide a path to permanent residence for certain young immigrants—both those here illegally and those whose parents are here on temporary visas and who will no longer be eligible when they become adults. The act sets out stringent conditions for eligibility. An individual must have arrived in the United States before age sixteen, lived here at least five years, and graduated from an American high school or obtained a GED. Those eligible would receive conditional permanent residency for six years, and would then be required to go on to attend college for at least two years or to perform two years of military service. They would also be required to demonstrate good moral character, a stringent legal standard that disqualifies an individual for most criminal offenses, providing false information on documents, or failing to register for Selective Service. At the end of six years, if all these conditions are met, the individual would be eligible for permanent residence.

The DREAM Act is no amnesty. It offers to young people who had no responsibility for their parents' initial decision to bring them into the United States the opportunity to earn their way to remain here. *As such, the Task Force supports passage of the DREAM Act, and believes that it provides a good framework for a broader legalization scheme.*

Extending such a scheme to adults who were fully responsible for their decision to come to the United States, and are already working here, produces an extra layer of complexity. Such individuals cannot be expected to earn their legal residency through schooling or military service. But Congress has already considered a number of sound alternatives. The McCain-Kennedy legislation, for instance, would have required applicants to show a history of employment in the United States, to prove that they had paid taxes, to be in the process of studying English and learning about U.S. history and government, to pass criminal and security background checks, and to pay significant fines along with the application fee. Like the DREAM Act, it would have established a six-year probationary period before a green-card application were possible. Some other versions of the legislation have called for a demonstrated knowledge of English and the performance of community service. What is central to these approaches is that they require those seeking legalization to show a history of contribution to the United States through work and taxes, a commitment to remaining by learning English and adopting U.S. democratic values, and a willingness to pay some restitution. These are not the ingredients of an amnesty.

The Task Force recommends that Congress approve a program of earned legalization for illegal migrants in the United States, subject to appropriate penalties, waiting periods, background checks, evidence of moral character, and a commitment to full participation in American society by learning English and embracing American values.

EMPLOYMENT ENFORCEMENT

No scheme of immigration reform will succeed without tough, fair, and effective enforcement that actually curbs illegal migration; this was one of the lessons of the aftermath of the 1986 IRCA legislation. *The Task Force recommends a mandatory system for verifying those who are authorized to work in the United States. This is the single most effective and humane enforcement tool available to discourage illegal migration. Employers who use that system in good faith should be exempt from penalties, and those who refuse to comply should face much more stringent sanctions.* The Task Force agrees with the conclusion of the Jordan Commission more than a decade ago that work site verification and sanctions for violators are "the linchpin of a comprehensive strategy to reduce illegal immigration." The core elements for ensuring widespread compliance would be twofold:

– *A workable and reliable biometric electronic verification system.* To permit employers to check reliably on the immigration status of potential hires, those coming to the United States under temporary or provisional work visas should be issued biometric, tamperproof identification cards that authorize them to work. Green cards for permanent residents are already biometrically enabled. The system could be very similar to the existing US-VISIT scheme, in which all visas issued by the State Department are biometrically enabled, include digitized fingerprints and photograph, and are on a database read by U.S. Customs and Border Protection (CBP) officers on the visa holder's arrival at the U.S. port of entry. The US-VISIT system has virtually eliminated identity fraud in U.S. visas. American employers should be able to identify a temporary or provisional worker visa holder through a similar system. Coupled with stronger security measures for U.S. identification documents, employers should also be able to readily verify the employment eligibility of new hires.

– *Strengthening employer sanctions.* To be effective, sanctions against employers who knowingly hire undocumented foreign workers need to be strengthened. Under the 1986 IRCA, the first offense for an employer for knowingly hiring illegal aliens is a minimal administrative penalty, and the penalty for a second offense is also administrative. Only if there is a third offense is the employer subject to a misdemeanor criminal prosecution. To strengthen the employer sanctions, the penalties need to be more stringent. Administrative penalties would remain appropriate for a company that negligently hired unauthorized workers, but the first offense for knowingly doing so should be prosecuted as a misdemeanor. A second offense, or even a first offense involving a significant number of undocumented employees, would warrant prosecution as a felony. The increase in penalties, however, is premised on the creation of a reliable electronic verification system, the provision of clear guidance to employers, and a clearly identifiable biometric foreign worker ID. Given a greater level of visible enforcement and prosecution to achieve deterrence, the vast majority of U.S. businesses will comply with the law.

As part of an overall strengthening of employer sanction laws, Congress should also consider additional civil consequences, such as facilitating private lawsuits by injured competitors by providing for treble damages against employers who hire illegal workers, on the grounds that this represents unfair competition. Such a law permitting private civil suits would assist in keeping a level playing field in particular business sectors and markets. For example, a meatpacker who is complying with the law would likely be more vigilant in monitoring competitors who are not if the law allowed him to sue a competitor using illegal labor. A similar approach has been used to augment criminal sanctions to achieve greater compliance with antitrust laws.

– *Verify in exchange for immunity.* An employer who verifies a new hire against the government's electronic database would gain immunity from prosecution. The tougher sanctions will motivate employers to install a system that connects with E-Verify. And because using the database will be enough for an employer to gain immunity, the burden will be on the government to make sure the system is accurate and fraud-proof.

— *Adequate resources to enforce the law.* The government must support the development of an electronic verification system that reads biometrics, not just Social Security numbers. ICE investigative resources also need to be adequate to achieve the type of deterrence enforcement that facilitates widespread compliance and to take on employers that resist compliance.

The government should be far more aggressive in identifying and penalizing employers who choose to willfully violate the law by continuing to hire unauthorized workers. The preferred tools should be large fines and, where appropriate, criminal penalties. Large-scale enforcement raids have had unfortunate humanitarian consequences and have hurt America's image abroad. Such raids should be carried out in a lower-profile manner than has sometimes been the case, with the primary goal of gathering evidence for prosecution of employers. Illegal workers arrested through worksite enforcement should certainly be put into removal proceedings, but the raids should be used primarily to punish employers who continue to rely on an unauthorized workforce. The Task Force is encouraged by the signals that the Obama administration is moving in this direction.

BORDER ENFORCEMENT

Border enforcement should be seen primarily as a tool for keeping out terrorists, serious criminals, and others who would harm the United States, but doing so in a way that does not damage legitimate cross-border commerce and movement of people. Although border enforcement is also an important part of discouraging illegal immigration, the country cannot rely on border enforcement measures alone to do so. Enormous strides have been made in recent years in gaining greater control over U.S. borders, and those efforts should be continued.

The Task Force supports the central elements of the Secure Border Initiative, including increased manpower for the U.S. Border Patrol and the creation of a virtual border, in which remote sensing gives the United States far greater visibility over who and what is crossing its land borders. By deploying detection technologies—from cameras to sensors to aerial vehicles—that give the United States full visibility over its southern border, the government will for the first time be able to get an accurate reading on how many unauthorized crossings of the border are taking place. Such information is critical to ultimately stemming the flow of illegal migrants, and will pay benefits in other areas such as curbing drug smuggling and controlling violence in the border region. Although initial trials of the new technologies have run into operational difficulties, they appear to be surmountable. *The Task Force recommends that DHS continue implementing the Secure Border Initiative, with its goal of gaining greater operational control over U.S. land borders.*

The Task Force is skeptical, however, of the security value of additional fencing along the Mexican border. Fencing is necessary in certain populated areas to prevent illegal border crossers from quickly disappearing into the local population, but it is of much less value in remote regions where it can more easily be skirted, though sometimes vehicle barriers can be a useful addition to security. What must be weighed in future decisions on fencing is whether the costs—both monetary and in the negative symbolism of an open country like the United States building huge fences on its border—are outweighed by the security benefits. In most cases those costs argue against any expansion beyond the 670 miles already authorized.

As discussed, the Task Force also supports smart border initiatives that use information technologies and targeting tools to help distinguish individuals who may pose a threat to the United States from the vast majority of legitimate visitors and immigrants. *The Task Force urges the administration to continue investing in improvements that allow scarce U.S. resources to be focused on the greatest threats.* Registered traveler programs, the NEXUS and SENTRI lanes at the land borders to speed the entry of frequent crossers who have undergone background checks, and other measures that expedite cross-border travel for known and trusted individuals should be encouraged and expanded. Such expansion has been impeded by inconsistent standards regarding which travelers are eligible for the program and the criteria for remaining in the program. These standards should be clarified and implemented with appropriate discretion following risk management principles.

Balancing security and openness has been especially difficult given the cramped, inadequate facilities at some of America's legal ports of entry, especially at the land borders. New investments in border infrastructure and manpower are needed to reduce delays at the entry ports yet allow for necessary inspections of those crossing the border. The economic stimulus bill makes an encouraging start by allocating more than $700 million to improvements at the land ports of entry on the U.S. borders with Canada and Mexico. Associated staffing needs must also be addressed immediately.

STATE AND LOCAL ENFORCEMENT

Enforcement of immigration laws is fundamentally a federal responsibility, but state and local police forces can and should augment those capabilities as long as it does not interfere with their core mission of maintaining safety and security in the communities they serve. To some extent, the controversy over state and local enforcement of immigration laws will be alleviated as a result of immigration reform that dramatically reduces the number of illegal immigrants in the country. *As a guiding principle, the Task Force recommends that state and local police forces not be involved in routine immigration enforcement, which could interfere with their other missions. On the other hand, state and local police forces should enter into agreements with the federal government that permit local officials to check the immigration status of individuals they arrest for serious crimes, which can enhance their law enforcement capabilities. Appropriate federal funding, personnel, and training must be provided to state and local agencies that choose to enter into these agreements.* State and local law enforcement should be barred from reporting the status of any immigrant with whom they come into contact because that person is a victim of a crime, a witness to a crime, or seeking emergency medical services. No state or local policy, however, should prevent law enforcement officials from reporting the immigration status of someone arrested for or convicted of a felony or other serious crime.

This is also an area in which additional consultation with the communities most affected by immigration enforcement would be extremely valuable. To help reconcile national-level goals of immigration reform with the local tensions that result, local trust- and consensus-building processes should be cultivated, perhaps with the help of conflict resolution organizations that could aid communities in coming to agreement on the best ways to balance immigration enforcement with the other priorities of local and state police.

ONGOING ISSUES

SCIENTIFIC COLLABORATION

Increasing America's openness to skilled foreign immigrants, particularly those with scientific and engineering talent, is critical for U.S. national security. Science is a global enterprise and thrives wherever the environment is most open to collaboration involving the best minds from around the world. While the United States still enjoys many advantages as the center for such collaborative work, the competition is increasing. Unnecessary visa and other restrictions diminish America's already shrinking advantage. The National Research Council argued this point recently: "Traditionally, the United States had to worry about science and technology flowing out of the country. Under today's conditions, the U.S. must make sure that advanced science and technology will continue to *flow* into the country." The United States, it urged, needs to "recognize the interdependence of national security and economic competitiveness." The default position should be openness and engagement "unless a compelling case can be made for restrictions."[136] The Task Force agrees.

With respect to visa policies, the State Department has made significant progress in trying to ensure that visa applications by scientists and foreign students are given priority and processed rapidly. There are encouraging signs that the Obama administration will improve the background screening system to ensure that visa decisions are made in a more timely fashion, but without increasing security risks. *The Task Force urges the continuation of efforts to streamline the background check process for granting visas to scientists and students, and in particular recommends that the Visas Mantis and "deemed export" procedures be used judiciously, and only for those working in fields that represent a genuine national security concern. The Task Force also favors more direct interaction with U.S. universities by the Visa Office of the State Department in resolving any technology-related disclosure or security concerns. Presently, many university officials are excluded from the process, and the redress mechanisms are not timely enough.*

MILITARY RECRUITING

Immigrants and their offspring are important potential recruits for the U.S. armed forces. The war against terrorism has forced the United States to become engaged either directly or indirectly in environments where language skills, cultural knowledge, and the ability to work with local populations are vital ingredients of military success.[137] Recruiting within the diverse immigrant populations of the United States is the most promising avenue for the armed forces to build up those capabilities. Yet policy restrictions have generally prevented recruiting anyone living in the United States who is not either a citizen or a green-card holder, even though there are now millions of potential immigrants, and their children, living here for long periods in temporary status.

One particularly promising pool of recruits includes the many young people whose parents are living in the United States on temporary work visas. Ordinarily, these young people lose their nonimmigrant status at age twenty-one unless they secure student or work visas. Yet often these young people have spent many years in America and have been educated here. Military service should be but is now largely not an option for them. Similarly, though the United States has a history in wartime of recruiting noncitizens abroad who can make valuable contributions to the armed forces, and offering them a quicker path to U.S. citizenship, that authority has not been used in recent conflicts. This makes particular sense for individuals who speak languages desperately needed to help the military in current conflicts (Arabic, Pashto, and so on) and who have already demonstrated their loyalty by working closely with the United States during those missions. These unnecessary restrictions work against U.S. security interests. The government has recently launched a pilot project to recruit up to one thousand people in lawful status, but has limited the pool to those with specialized medical or language skills.

The Task Force recommends that the administration permit a broader recruiting effort by the armed forces among noncitizens, with appropriate security safeguards. The U.S. armed forces should be allowed to recruit individuals who have lived in the United States for at least two years in some form of nonimmigrant status, as well as a limited number of foreign citizens who have provided exceptional service to the U.S. armed forces abroad.

IMPROVING AMERICA'S IMAGE

Travel to the United States, cross-border exchanges, and other efforts that allow a greater number of foreigners to see the country for themselves are among the best public diplomacy tools the United States has. The U.S. government needs to use them more fully and remove unnecessary impediments to travel.

In its January 2008 report, the Secure Borders and Open Doors Advisory Committee, established by former secretary of homeland security Michael Chertoff and former secretary of state Condoleezza Rice, made forty-four recommendations to facilitate travel to the United States. Some of these measures have been acted on by the different departments involved, including the expansion of programs to speed arrival by frequent travelers such as the NEXUS and SENTRI programs, and improvements in visa processing. But many of the core recommendations continue to languish, even as the government is pushing ahead with ambitious new programs aimed at closely monitoring the arrival and departure of travelers from the United States. The committee co-chairs have urged cabinet and presidential-level attention to the larger issue of finding the right balance between security and openness.[138]

The Task Force recommends that the administration and Congress take a comprehensive look at the current security-related restrictions on travel to the United States, with an eye toward lifting restrictions that do not significantly reduce the risk of terrorists or serious criminals entering the country. As a start, we urge the government to move forward in implementing the remainder of the SBODAC recommendations.

Several important SBODAC recommendations have yet to be implemented:

– the resumption of domestic reissuance of visas for business nonimmigrant visitors, and its extension to foreign students and exchange visitors, which would allow holders of these visas to remain in the United States without the expense and difficulty of returning home to renew their visas;

– the expansion of consular posts abroad and continued development of videoconferencing to ease the visa application process; and

– the expansion of the U.S. International Registered Traveler program to speed entry by frequent visitors to the United States.

Several additional steps, however, should be considered beyond the SBODAC report. After 9/11, the United States set up special screening procedures for most male visa applicants from a list of roughly two dozen predominantly Muslim and Arab countries. The system, known as the National Security Entry-Exit Registration System, collected extensive information and added additional background checks before visas could be granted to these applicants, and required these individuals to undergo secondary inspection every time they arrive in the United States and at specified intervals during their time in the country. NSEERS also applied to citizens of those countries already living in the United States. The program was scaled back in 2003 after the Department of Homeland Security concluded that it was of little value in identifying and keeping terrorists out of the country. The National Commission on Terrorist Attacks Upon the United States (the 9/11 Commission) also concluded that the program demonstrated few benefits from a counterterrorism perspective.[139] The vestiges of the program still bedevil those who are caught up in it. Given that the program has been made redundant by other security measures, *the Task Force recommends that the special NSEERS requirements for male visa applicants from Muslim and Arab countries be eliminated as soon as possible. U.S. consular officers and border inspectors, however, should continue to have the flexibility to require additional background checks or other inspection measures wherever they deem appropriate.*

Congress should also consider reversing legislation passed in 2004 that makes mandatory what was previously optional: that State Department consular officers conduct personal interviews before granting a visa to would-be travelers to the United States. The mandatory requirement, in many cases where biometrics have already been obtained from the applicant and remain available for database checks, wastes scarce consular resources on low-risk travelers and increases the costs and difficulty for many potential visitors. This is particularly so in large countries like Brazil, India, and China, where an individual might have to travel hundreds of miles to the nearest U.S. embassy or consulate for what is often a perfunctory interview. *The Task Force recommends that Congress lift the mandatory interview requirement and restore the discretion of State Department consular officers to waive interviews when warranted, based on the application of sound risk management principles.*

Finally, although efforts have been made to promote courtesy and a welcoming spirit into the frontline border agency, too many visitors to the United States are simply poorly treated when they arrive, either through lengthy delays in secondary inspection or needlessly brusque treatment by border inspectors. Because this is often the only contact that foreign citizens have with U.S. government authority, it conveys an unnecessarily poor image of the United States. The difficulty of the job facing U.S. border inspectors cannot be overestimated. They see themselves rightly as constituting a last line of defense for keeping terrorists out of the country, and since 9/11 their mission has been defined overwhelmingly by the importance of that task. *The Task Force recommends a clear message from the highest level of the government that the responsibility of border inspectors is a dual one, and that treating the vast majority of law-abiding visitors to the United States with dignity and fairness is as important as keeping out those who do not belong here.*

UPHOLDING AMERICAN VALUES

Even as the United States enforces its immigration laws vigorously, it is vital that this be done in a way that upholds core American values, humane treatment, and the dignity of the individual. *The Task Force believes three areas in particular are in need of immediate and serious review: incarceration policies, the severe penalties for some immigration and minor criminal violations, and policies on refugees and asylees.*

The Task Force believes that all immigrants to the United States, regardless of their legal status, have a right to fair consideration under the law and humane treatment. We therefore encourage the administration and Congress to implement the following measures:

1. *Expand the use of alternatives to detention.* Pilot projects in DHS have shown that programs that provide an alternative to incarceration— from restrictive measures such as ankle bracelets to less restrictive measures that are the equivalent of monitoring parolees—are

successful in many instances at keeping track of asylum claimants or others facing removal hearings, and at lower costs than incarceration. Although any individual considered a criminal or a security threat should be detained for as long as necessary, except in a few cases, asylum claimants or immigration violators are not who would ordinarily be thought of as criminals and should not be treated as such.

That same principle also calls for better treatment of those detained while they await deportation or adjudication of legal challenges or asylum requests. Those who must be detained for security reasons should be housed in facilities separate from regular criminal populations and as close as possible to their family and community, provided with safe and healthy living conditions, and given full access to medical treatment when necessary. Detainees should also be allowed ready access to legal counsel (and interpreters if needed), which in most cases is necessary for individuals trying to deal with the complexities of U.S. immigration law. Their terms of detention should be kept as short as possible.

2. *Revisit some of the penalties passed by Congress as part of the Antiterrorism and Effective Death Penalty Act of 1996 and the Illegal Immigration Reform and Immigrant Responsibility Act of 1996.* Congress should reconsider provisions of the 1996 laws that instituted mandatory three-year, five-year, ten-year, and permanent bans from the United States for certain violations of U.S. immigration law. Too often these bars on admission, rather than deterring people from remaining illegally in the United States, have posed an insurmountable hurdle to those who might otherwise be able to obtain lawful status by going abroad and applying for reentry. Although such provisions have their place, they should not always be mandatory, and there should be discretion for immigration officers and the immigration courts to waive them when appropriate. Congress should also clarify the meaning of the term *aggravated felony* so as to limit mandatory deportations to those found guilty of serious crimes, especially crimes of violence, and to clarify the situations in which U.S. attorneys and immigration judges will be allowed to consider alternative penalties.

For its part, the administration should increase the discretion of immigration trial counsel to halt deportation proceedings in certain cases. Before 9/11, government immigration lawyers had—and were encouraged—to exercise discretion to not seek deportation orders against unlawful immigrants in cases in which it would cause severe hardship for their families or for other humanitarian reasons. That discretion should be restored. Immigration judges should also have the ability to consider extenuating circumstances such as the nature of the offense, the time since it occurred, and an individual's family ties to the United States in making decisions on cases involving aggravated felonies.

3. *The administration should create an office within DHS that is responsible for refugee protection, and give greater priority for refugee issues through-out DHS and in the White House.* As recommended, the government should limit detention of asylum seekers, wherever it is consistent with security needs, and establish better treatment for those who must be detained. Congress must revisit the broad definitions of material support for terrorist organizations that were approved after 9/11 to ensure that those laws better target persons with genuine terrorist ties or who have voluntarily aided and assisted terrorist organizations. The government should also support efforts to rescue academic scholars facing persecution in their home countries.

Further, the Task Force supports the recommendations of the United States Commission on International Religious Freedom, which calls for improvements in the treatment of asylum seekers who face expedited removal when they make their claims at a U.S. port of entry.[140]

Finally, the Task Force recommends the creation of a new non-immigrant visa category for endangered and persecuted scholars, which would significantly increase the U.S. capacity not only to protect lives but also to bring to this country some of the world's most brilliant minds.

DEVELOPMENT

Permitting migration from developing countries is one of the more effective ways that the United States encourages development in poorer countries. The substantial increase in incomes for those who move here from developing countries, much of which is returned home as remittances, makes a significant contribution to alleviating poverty and developing the economy. In addition, many migrants to the United States, particularly those who come initially as students, return home with knowledge, skills, and contacts in the United States that are extremely valuable for economic and political progress in their home countries. *The Task Force believes that the best contribution U.S. immigration policy can make to development in poorer countries is the establishment of policies that offer generous opportunities for both skilled and unskilled migrants to come to work in the United States.*

Ultimately, however, the goal of the United States is to see development take hold in poorer countries so that new job opportunities are created that reduce the pressure to migrate. Although emigration can yield tremendous economic benefits for some in poor countries, it has some negative consequences—often including splitting families—and is an option only available to certain persons, usually not the destitute. *The Task Force urges the U.S. government to work with major sending countries to address the core development issues whose resolution would allow the benefits of migration to be most fully realized, to take a more systematic look at the impact of U.S. immigration policies on development, and to begin factoring immigration concerns into trade and aid policies aimed at lifting living standards in poorer countries.*

RELATIONS WITH MEXICO

As discussed, there are reasons to believe that some of the pressures that have led to very high levels of migration from Mexico to the United States will abate, though the consequences of the current weakness in both the U.S. and Mexican economies are difficult to forecast. Even if immigration from Mexico does slow, the United States will never be able to establish and maintain an orderly system for managing migration flows without closer cooperation with Mexico. Mexico is a special case in U.S. immigration policy, and needs to be treated as such. Yet the failure of the efforts of former presidents Fox and Bush to conclude a bilateral accord on migration has left both sides understandably wary of another effort. There will need to be a gradual rebuilding of trust on both sides of the border.

In the longer run, the lasting solution to the problem of illegal immigration from Mexico is faster, sustainable economic growth in Mexico that reduces the huge income disparities between the two countries, and creates jobs for the vast majority of Mexicans who would rather stay at home. The North American Free Trade Agreement has been an important contributor to Mexican growth. Trade between the United States and Mexico has nearly tripled since the agreement came into force. But there is still a long way to go. *The Task Force recommends that the United States take additional steps to encourage economic growth in Mexico, and in particular work to remove border-related impediments to trade.*[141] *It also recommends an expansion of occupational categories allowed for Trade NAFTA visas under the North American Free Trade Agreement to Mexican and Canadian citizens.*

The United States, for instance, should be investing more in the infrastructure at the legal ports of entry, and hiring additional CBP inspectors, to ensure that delays in cross-border trade are not discouraging investment in Mexico. The current trade dispute over rules regarding Mexican trucks operating on American roads has done needless damage to cross-border trade at a time when neither country can afford it; the dispute should be resolved quickly and finally in a way that expedites commerce but maintains the safety of vehicles on American roads. Away from the border, the U.S. government should consider increased development aid targeted at poorer communities in Mexico that are the source of many illegal migrants to the United States. None of these measures is a panacea, but the United States has a strong interest in exploring all reasonable means to strengthen the economy of its southern neighbor.

In addition, Mexico and the United States have mutual interests in cooperating on immigration and security issues. Each has a stake in orderly management of the border that both allows legitimate commerce and cross-border travelers to move quickly between the two countries and protects each country from external and internal threats.

Partly as a consequence of growing violence in the border region, security cooperation is becoming increasingly central to U.S.-Mexico relations. The $1.4 billion Merida Initiative to assist Mexico in its fight against the powerful drug cartels is a milestone, and both sides should build on that initiative. The United States has recently acknowledged its own responsibility for the drug crisis, and has pledged new measures to try to stem the flow of arms and laundered cash from the United States into Mexico, and to reduce domestic demand for illegal drugs. Efforts to tackle the drug crisis have produced closer binational cooperation, particularly at the military level, than has been seen before. If successful, these efforts may begin to erode some of the wariness, especially on the Mexican side, that has been an obstacle to closer collaboration. The Council on Foreign Relations' recent Independent Task Force report, *U.S.-Latin America Relations: A New Direction for a New Reality,* for instance, called for closer cooperation between U.S. and Mexican law enforcement authorities in interdicting the human smuggling networks that operate across the border as well as in tackling the problem of drug smuggling. The United States and Mexico have also cooperated extremely closely to prevent terrorists from transiting Mexican territory en route to the United States, and both governments should build on these efforts.

Ultimately, however, resolving the immigration issue needs to start with the United States reforming its own immigration laws and practices. *The Task Force believes that the most important positive signal that the United States can send to Mexico is to broaden the current narrow focus on enforcement, and to reengage with the issue of comprehensive immigration reform.* Mexico and the United States would be the biggest beneficiaries of immigration reform, by providing new legal channels for Mexicans to live and work in the United States, offering a path to legalization for millions of Mexicans already in the United States, and reducing the security risks of the status quo.

Conclusion: Maintaining the Focus

This Task Force report has attempted two things. First, it has tried to show why America's national interests require a better immigration policy that will help the United States enhance its economic, diplomatic, and military standing in the world. Second, it has argued that comprehensive immigration reform, coupled with new investments to improve the functioning of the U.S. legal immigration system and ensure effective enforcement of immigration laws, are necessary to achieve that end. *To reiterate the Task Force's vision, we believe the United States must generously welcome immigrants through an orderly and efficient legal system, must enforce sensible and understandable visa and immigration laws that welcome both permanent immigrants and temporary visitors, and must effectively control and secure its borders, denying entry to those who are not permitted and denying jobs to those not authorized to work here.* Despite the very real difficulties that will have to be surmounted to pass legislation and create a more efficient and effective immigration system, the Task Force believes that a historic opportunity exists to make such improvements.

The passage of new immigration reform legislation by Congress along the principles outlined in this report would be a major accomplishment. But, as the history of repeated rounds of immigration legislation has demonstrated, immigration is not an issue that can simply be revisited every decade or so and then forgotten. Immigration policy is simply too important to a broad range of U.S. interests, both foreign and domestic, to be considered in such a sporadic fashion. The list of issues discussed—some of which are long-standing problems but others of which have emerged only in the past few years—demonstrates why immigration policy must receive regular attention and action by any U.S. administration and the Congress.

More than a decade ago, the Commission for the Study of International Migration and Cooperative Development, created by Congress after the passage of IRCA in 1986, urged that "a government structure be devised to assure that the issue of migration policy receive as much attention as do the consuming but often transient day-to-day concerns that otherwise dominate the process." Since then, the structure of immigration policymaking has been overhauled with the creation of the Department of Homeland Security, but the fundamental problem remains. Immigration is still an issue that is considered only sporadically important, rather than one that is vital to America's well-being as a nation. That must change.

The Task Force considered, but does not recommend, any significant structural changes in the U.S. government apparatus for handling immigration policy. The Department of Homeland Security is a new organization that has undergone many growing pains, and a fresh round of reorganization would likely create more problems than it solves. Instead, it is simply time for the administration and Congress to treat immigration policy as an issue that requires regular attention.

The Task Force recommends that immigration policy be an ongoing subject of administration and congressional management. The creation of a Standing Commission on Immigration and Labor Markets would be a positive step in that direction, forcing Congress and the administration to deal regularly, rather than sporadically, with some of the major elements of immigration policy. New congressional appropriations to speed the transformation of the legal immigration system into a modern, efficient bureaucracy would create greater ongoing congressional oversight of the operation of U.S. Citizenship and Immigration Services. Congress is already vigilant in monitoring the administration's efforts to keep bad people out of the country through border security and immigration enforcement, and needs to be equally vigilant in monitoring its efforts to bring good people in.

Both Congress and the administration need to consider on an ongoing basis the broad range of immigration and border policies, and to be certain they are factored appropriately into both foreign and domestic policy. Immigration policy should be on the table not only at the Domestic Policy Council in the White House, where it has historically been considered, but also at the National Economic Council (NEC) and the National Security Council (NSC). Given the critical role that immigration policy plays in the economic competitiveness of the United States and its long-run military security, these issues must be on the agenda at the highest levels of the administration. The recent plan by the Obama White House to create a new position on the NSC staff responsible for U.S. strategies on global engagement is an encouraging step in this direction.

As written at the outset of this report, how America handles its immigration policy is vital to its standing in the world, and the failure to make significant improvements will have repercussions for years to come. Immigration has long been a secret to America's success, and no issue will be more important for its success in the future. The administration and Congress have an opportunity to put the country's immigration policy on a path to that future. This Task Force urges them to seize it.

Additional or Dissenting Views

The report is timely and needed, and I concur with most of the recommendations. I would add the following, however: first, the report fails to discuss the long-standing U.S. practice of granting citizenship automatically to almost anyone born in the United States, regardless of their parents' status (the exception being children of diplomats). I believe as a policy matter the United States should not extend citizenship to children born in our country to parents who are here illegally. The current practice invites illegal migration, promotes public cynicism, and is often the only basis for the cry of family separation when the parents are deported. Besides Canada, the United States is the only Western nation allowing birthright citizenship for children of illegal aliens. This practice could probably be changed by Congress (I would not make it retroactive) without a constitutional amendment, but I would favor such an amendment if absolutely necessary.

Second, I believe the United States should adopt a points system for identifying and prioritizing immigration by skilled workers, though without sacrificing the beneficial aspects of the U.S. visa system that allow companies to seek out and sponsor foreign workers. Canada, Australia, and New Zealand have been able to implement such systems successfully. There should be no quota for certain highly skilled jobs that are deemed critical to our economy, and for other highly skilled jobs that are needed, the quota should be significantly larger than the current H-1B visa cap. The tasks of identifying needed jobs and setting caps would be appropriate for the new Standing Commission on Immigration and Labor Markets recommended by the Task Force.

Third, as we shift the focus of immigrant visas to workers needed for our economy and away from family preferences, I favor limiting family preferences to the spouses and minor children of citizens or green-card holders. I would eliminate preferences for siblings and adult children. Finally, I believe our current system for processing asylum claims is generally adequate and that the standard should be to meet our treaty obligations in good faith, not to establish "the highest standards of due process," as the report argues.

Robert C. Bonner

Proposals for immigration policy reform increasingly focus on the need to gain control and impose order. Orderly entry and exit of visitors and immigrants to the United States is an important objective, as the Task Force report rightly argues. But it is important also to understand that some of those who seek to enter the United States are in an inherently disorderly situation. Refugees are in many respects involuntary migrants. Forced to flee their home countries, upend their lives, and abandon loved ones, homes, and careers, they often must make a hasty exit without the benefit of official government permission, travel papers, or entry visas. That is the refugee experience; it is by definition chaotic. While we can and should seek to impose as much regularity as possible on the adjudication of refugee claims, we also must take care not to penalize refugees for, essentially, being refugees. The current system of expedited removal and mandatory detention has worked an extraordinary hardship on many deserving refugees. Expedited removal—a process built on the backwards assumption that asylum seekers who fail to present valid travel documents are prima facie ineligible for refugee protection—poses an insurmountable hurdle for many and has resulted in the United States erroneously returning refugees into the very authorities from whom they fled in fear. And the widespread and growing resort to detention of asylum seekers in immigration jails without judicial oversight has raised questions about U.S. compliance with its human rights obligations under the international refugee protection treaty, which it led the world in drafting and to which it is a party. See Human Rights First, *U.S. Detention of Asylum Seekers: Seeking Protection, Finding Prison* (April 2009). The United States should consider the impact of such policies, not only on the refugees directly affected by them, but on broader U.S. foreign policy interests. For better or worse, the United States sets the standard for reasonable and humane treatment of migrants around the world. If the United States endorses harsh treatment of immigrants, it erodes the norms designed to protect them, and other countries will have license to do the same. Treatment of immigrants and refugees is one of many areas in which the United States sets the example for the rest of the world. It needs to be a better one.

Elisa Massimino

I agree with the report's conclusion that border and immigration restrictions used in a targeted and focused way are important to our nation's security. But that is not true of the misdirected enforcement efforts of the last two decades that have tended to focus on farmworkers, nannies, gardeners, and factory workers instead of legitimate national security concerns. For this reason, although the recent extraordinary border enforcement efforts have, indeed, been "impressive," they have not been effective or beneficial. Similarly, increasingly aggressive *internal* enforcement efforts—such as raids and local police enforcement of immigration—have undermined traditional American values and created a hostile environment, but have not made us safer.

The outsized enforcement budgets have created an imbalance where immigration violations are far more aggressively enforced than other workplace violations. Focusing resources on wage and hour and health and safety violations would be far more beneficial for U.S. workers. Implementation of a more viable legal immigration system would relieve the pressure on border and interior enforcement alike, reducing the need for expensive and divisive immigration enforcement measures. Failure to address future migration flows was the real lesson of the 1986 amnesty.

With respect to which, it is inaccurate to characterize our experience with temporary worker schemes as "mixed." Disastrous is a better word, at least with respect to lower-skilled jobs. Therefore, I am pleased the report endorses the idea of a commission to reshape future flows. The AFL-CIO and Change to Win union federations have endorsed a similar commission to improve the match between immigration policies and the changing economy.

Eliseo Medina

The report of the Task Force is well reasoned and sensitively delineates the complexity of the immigration policy challenges faced in the

United States. I would disagree with or add to several of the recommendations, however.

The idea for a Standing Commission on Immigration and Labor Markets remains too amorphous conceptually. Sufficient oversight and enforcement of current labor protections must be a critical goal, but such a commission would add a layer of national-level determinations of local labor market needs. This would make the system more complex rather than serving the report's stated goal of simplification. Mechanisms already exist to identify locally determined labor needs, and these would have merited further consideration.

The report needed greater focus on issues at the legal ports of entry, where staffing is still woefully short and attrition has eroded the collective experience of CBP officers. It is predictable that port officers are less than welcoming to visitors when they have inadequate staffing support, too little time for training, and tremendous increasing demands. Also, specialists in immigration, customs, and agriculture laws should be available 24/7 at the ports of entry.

Further, as noted in the report, enforcement-only approaches do not help either our security or the economy. Such approaches have also eroded the long-standing use of prosecutorial discretion in dealing with immigration offenses. Operation Streamline, for example, has clogged the federal courts with first-time misdemeanor offenders, weakening due process protections without improving border security. I agree with the report's core recommendation that rational reform of immigration laws in concert with security measures is a better way to reduce illegal border crossings.

Finally, the report is too sanguine about the effects of expanding section 287(g) agreements. Numerous law enforcement associations support preserving the line between federal civil immigration law enforcement and state and local criminal law enforcement. Any expansion or endorsement of 287(g) programs or their Criminal Alien Program companions must be limited to felony violations. Otherwise, security in local communities will not be enhanced.

Kathleen Campbell Walker

Endnotes

1. Antonio Spilimbergo, "Democracy and Foreign Education" (IMF working paper no. 07/51, March 2007).
2. World Bank, "Remittance Flows to Developing Countries Are Estimated to Exceed $300 Billion in 2008," http://peoplemove.worldbank.org/en/content/remittance-flows-to-developing-countries.
3. Apprehension rates at the southern border, which are used by the Border Patrol as a rough measure of the level of illegal migration across the land border, have fallen to their lowest levels since the 1970s. See Richard Marosi, "Border Arrests Drop to 1970s Levels," *Los Angeles Times*, March 8, 2009; see also Jeffrey S. Passel and D'Vera Cohn, "Trends in Unauthorized Immigration: Undocumented Inflow Now Trails Legal Inflow" (report, Pew Hispanic Center, October 2, 2008), http://www.pewhispanic.org/files/reports/94.pdf.
4. See for instance, Thelma Gutierrez and Wayne Drash, "Bad economy forcing immigrants to reconsider U.S.," CNN.com, February 10, 2009. Research, however, suggests no definitive evidence yet that illegal immigrants are returning home either as a result of the slowing U.S. economy or increased interior enforcement. See Demetrios G. Papademetriou and Aaron Terrazas, "Immigrants and the Current Economic Crisis: Research Evidence, Policy Challenges, and Implications" (report, Migration Policy Institute, January 2009), http://www.migrationpolicy.org/pubs/lmi_recessionJan09.pdf.
5. David L. Bartlett, "U.S. Immigration Policy in Global Perspective: International Migration in OECD Countries" (special report, Immigration Policy Center, Winter 2007).
6. Senate Committee on the Judiciary, Subcommittee on Immigration, Citizenship, Refugees, Border Security and International Law, "The Role of Immigrants in the U.S. Labor Market," testimony by Peter R. Orszag, 110th Cong. 1st sess., May 3, 2007.
7. George Borjas has argued that immigration to the United States between 1980 and 2000 reduced the wages of native workers by 3 percent, and wages of the least educated workers by 9 percent. But other economists have come up with quite different figures, estimating a 2 percent gain for all native workers and only a 1 percent decline for the least educated. See George Borjas, "The Labor Demand Curve is Downward Sloping: Reexamining the Impact of Immigration on the Labor Market," *Quarterly Journal of Economics* vol. 118, no. 4 (2003), pp. 1333–74; David Card, "Is the New Immigration Really So Bad?" *Economic Journal* vol. 115, no. 507 (2005), pp. F300-F323; Gianmarco Ottaviano and Giovanni Peri, "Rethinking the Effects of Immigration on Wages" (NBER Working Paper No. 12497, July 2006); see also the excellent overview of the debate in Roger Lowenstein, "The Immigration Equation," *New York Times Magazine*, July 9, 2006.

8. Senate Committee on the Judiciary, "The Role of Immigrants in the U.S. Labor Market," p. 3.

9. Nicholas Eberstadt, "Born in the USA," *The American Interest*, Summer 2007.

10. United Nations Population Division, "Replacement Migration: Is it a Solution to Declining and Aging Populations?" (New York: UN Publication Office, 2002).

11. U.S. Bureau of Labor Statistics, "Occupational Outlook Handbook, 2008–2009 Edition," http://data.bls.gov/cgi-bin/print.pl/oco/oco2003.htm.

12. Compiled from American Communities Survey, 2007 data, http://www.lpums.org.

13. Michael Fix, Randolph Capps, and Katrina Fortuny, "Trends in the Low-Wage Immigrant Labor Force, 2000–2005" (report, The Urban Institute, March 2007), http://www.urban.org/url.cfm?ID=411426.

14. See the powerful recent study by Peter B. Dixon and Maureen T. Rimmer, "Illegal Immigration: Restrict or Liberalize" (Center of Policy Studies, Monash University, April 2009), which uses economy-wide models to estimate the welfare costs of legalizing illegal immigrants in the United States versus turning them away through tougher enforcement. It concludes that restricting the inflow of illegal immigrants "biases the occupational mix of employment for U.S. workers toward low-paid, low-skilled jobs" (p. 3), which would have significant negative impacts on overall U.S. economic welfare.

15. Bartlett, "U.S. Immigration Policy in Global Perspective," p. 5.

16. Elizabeth Collett, "The Proposed European Blue Card System: Arming for the Global War for Talent?" *Migration Information Source*, January 7, 2008, http://www.migrationinformation.org/feature/display.cfm?ID=667.

17. Demetrios G. Papademetriou, "Selecting Economic Stream Immigrants through Points Systems," *Migration Information Source*, May 18, 2007, http://www.migrationinformation.org/Feature/display.cfm?id=602.

18. Kirk Semple, "Applications for Foreign Worker Visas Are Down," *New York Times*, April 9, 2009.

19. Government Accountability Office, "Higher Education: Challenges in Attracting International Students to the United States and Implications for Global Competitiveness," statement of George A. Scott, director of Education, Workforce and Income Security Issues, 110th Cong. 1st sess., June 29, 2007, http://www.gao.gov/new.items/d071047t.pdf.

20. "Japanese Immigration: Don't Bring Me Your Huddled Masses," *The Economist*, December 30, 2008.

21. Rajika Bhandari and Peggy Blumenthal, "Global Student Mobility: Moving Towards Brain Exchange," in *The Europa World of Learning 2008*, vol. 1 (London: Routledge, 2008).

22. Cornelia Dean, "Scientists Fear Visa Trouble Will Drive Foreign Students Away," *New York Times*, March 3, 2009.

23. Norman R. Augustine, "Scilence," *Science,* September 19, 2008.

24. Jacob Funk Kirkegaard, *The Accelerating Decline in America's High-Skilled Workforce: Implications for Immigration Policy* (Washington, DC: Peterson Institute for International Economics, 2007).

25. Institute of International Education, *Open Doors 2008: Report on International Educational Exchange* (New York: Institute of International Education), http://www.opendoors.iienetwork.org/.

26. NAFSA: Association of International Educators, "International Education: The Neglected Dimension of Public Diplomacy," http://www.nafsa.org/_/Document/_/public_diplomacy_2008.pdf.

27. Susan K. Brown and Frank D. Bean, "Post 9/11 International Graduate Enrollment in

the United States: Unintended Consequences of National Security Strategies," in *Immigration Policy and Security: U.S., European and Commonwealth Perspectives*, eds. Terri E. Givens et al. (New York: Routledge, 2009).

28. NAFSA, "International Education: The Neglected Dimension of Public Diplomacy" (Washington, DC: Association of International Educators, 2008).

29. "Higher Education: The Future is Another Country," *The Economist*, December 30, 2008.

30. Jennifer Hunt and Marjolaine Gauthier-Loiselle, "How Much Does Immigration Boost Innovation?" (NBER Working Paper No. 14312, September 2008).

31. Gnanaraj Chellaraj, Keith E. Maskus, and Aaditya Mattoo, "The Contribution of Skilled Immigration and International Graduate Students to U.S. Innovation" (World Bank Policy Research Working Paper No. 3588, May 2005).

32. William R. Kerr and William F. Lincoln, "The Supply Side of Innovation: H-1B Visa Reforms and US Ethnic Invention" (Harvard Business School Working Paper No. 09-005, December 2008).

33. Vivek Wadhwa et al., "America's New Immigrant Entrepreneurs: Part I" (working paper, Duke University School of Engineering, January 4, 2007).

34. Doris Meissner, Deborah W. Meyers, Demetrios G. Papademetriou, and Michael Fix, "Immigration and America's Future: A New Chapter" (report, Independent Task Force on Immigration and America's Future, Migration Policy Institute, September 2006), p. 8.

35. See "ICE's Use of Immigration and Customs Authorities to Address National Security Threats: Examples," November 28, 2008, http://www.ice.gov/pi/news/factsheets/terrorismthreats.htm.

36. Donald Kerwin and Margaret D. Stock, "National Security and Immigration Policy: Reclaiming Terms, Measuring Success, and Setting Priorities" (report, U.S. Military Academy Combating Terrorism Center, West Point, June 2006).

37. Quoted in National Research Council, *Science and Security in a Post-9/11 World: A Report Based on Regional Discussions Between the Science and Security Communities* (Washington, DC: The National Academies Press, 2007).

38. National Research Council, *Beyond 'Fortress America': National Security Controls on Science and Technology in a Globalized World* (Washington, DC: The National Academies Press, 2009).

39. See, for instance, Pierre Chao, "Toward a U.S. Export Control and Technology Transfer System for the 21st Century" (Center for Strategic and International Studies, May 2008); John J. Hamre, Jay C. Farrar, and James A. Lewis, "Technology and Security in the 21st Century: U.S. Military Export Control Reform" (Center for Strategic and International Studies, May 2001).

40. Government Accountability Office, "Border Security: Improvements Needed to Reduce Time Taken to Adjudicate Visas for Science Students and Scholars," GAO 04-371 (Washington, DC: Goverment Printing Office, February 2004); "Border Security: Streamlined Visas Mantis Program has Lowered Burden on Foreign Science Students and Scholars, but Further Refinements Needed," GAO 05-198 (Washington, DC: Goverment Printing Office, February 2005).

41. Dean, "Scientists Fear Visa Trouble Will Drive Foreign Students Away."

42. See Robert H. Scales, *The Past and Present as Prologue: Future Warfare through the Lens of Contemporary Conflict* (Washington, DC: Center for a New American Security, April 2009).

43. Julia Preston, "U.S. Military Will Offer Path to Citizenship," *New York Times*, February 14, 2009.

44. "Global Public Opinion in the Bush Years (2001–2008)" (report, Pew Global Attitudes Project, December 18, 2008), http://pewglobal.org/reports/pdf/263.pdf.

45. House Committee on Foreign Affairs, Subcommittee on International Organizations, Human Rights and Oversight, "The Decline in America's Reputation: Why?" 110th Cong. 2d sess., June 11, 2008, Committee Print.

46. See "Changing Course: A New Direction for U.S. Relations with the Muslim World" (report, Leadership Group on U.S.-Muslim Engagement, September 2008); see also Richard L. Armitage and Joseph S. Nye Jr., "A Smarter, More Secure America" (report, CSIS Commission on Smart Power, Center for Strategic and International Studies, November 2007).

47. U.S. State Department, Bureau of Consular Affairs. Report of the Visa Office 2008, http://www.travel.state.gov/visa/frvi/statistics/statistics_4391.html.

48. Quoted in House Committee on Foreign Affairs, "The Decline in America's Reputation," p. 27.

49. Discover America Partnership/RT Strategies Survey of International Travelers, November 20, 2006.

50. According to Commerce Department figures, the United States had 25,341 million overseas visitors in 2008, some 633,000 fewer than in 2000. See U.S. Department of Commerce, International Trade Administration, Office of Travel and Tourism Industries, *International Visitation to the United States: A Statistical Summary of U.S. Arrivals (2008)*. The U.S. travel industry estimates that if the United States had maintained its share of international travel, it would have resulted in fifty-eight million more visitors, $182 billion in new spending, $27 billion in new tax revenue, and 245,000 more American jobs in 2008. See "U.S. Travel: Continued Shortfall in Overseas Arrivals to United States Since 9/11 Furthers America's Economic Crisis" (press release, U.S. Travel Association, March 24, 2009).

51. "Secure Borders and Open Doors: Preserving Our Welcome to the World in an Age of Terrorism" (report, Secure Borders and Open Doors Advisory Committee, U.S. Department of Homeland Security and State, January 2008), http://www.migrationpolicy.org/pubs/MPI_SBODAC_011608.pdf; see follow-up progress report dated October 29, 2008 and letter from SBODAC chairs John S. Chen and Jared L. Cohon to Secretary of State Condoleezza Rice and Secretary of Homeland Security Michael Chertoff, obtained by the Task Force project director.

52. "We polled young Arab leaders. These are people generally more favorable to the United States in the UAE. These are few hundred young men and women who are college educated, want to start a business etc., etc. We asked them, 'what do you need?' They told us the tools that they needed to start a business or expand their business. Where would you go? The United States. Why? Because that is the platinum standard. Where would you not? China and Japan. Why? Because we have no cultural affinity" (Committee on Foreign Affairs, Subcommittee on International Organizations, Human Rights and Oversight and the Subcommittee on the Western Hemisphere, testimony by John Zogby, 110th Cong., 1st sess., March 8, 2007, http://foreignaffairs.house.gov/110/33824.pdf).

53. A recent study by the Pew Research Center found that 73 percent of the children of unauthorized immigrant parents were born in the United States, and therefore by law are U.S. citizens (see Passel and Cohn, "A Portrait of Unauthorized Immigrants").

54. David A. Martin, "Twilight Statuses: A Closer Examination of the Unauthorized Population" (policy brief, Migration Policy Institute, June 2005).

55. "Immigration Enforcement Actions: 2007" (annual report, Office of Immigration Statistics, U.S. Department of Homeland Security, December 2008), http://www.dhs.gov/xlibrary/assets/statistics/publications/enforcement_ar_07.pdf.

56. Alison Siskin, Andorra Bruno, Blas Nunez-Neto, Lisa M. Seghetti, and Ruth Ellen Wasem, "Immigration Enforcement Within the United States," CRS report RL33351 (Washington, DC: Library of Congress, Congressional Research Service, April 6, 2006).

57. Doris Meissner and Donald Kerwin, *DHS and Immigration: Taking Stock and Correcting Course* (Washington, DC: Migration Policy Institute, 2009), p. 14.

58. Amy Goldstein and Dana Priest, "Careless Detention: Medical Care in Immigrant Prisons," *Washington Post*, May 11–14, 2008, http://www.washingtonpost.com/wp-srv/nation/specials/immigration/index.html.

59. According to Immigration and Customs Enforcement, its Intensive Supervision Appearance Program (ISAP), which includes electronic monitoring, home curfews, in-person reporting, and surprise home visits, has a 99 percent appearance rate at immigration hearings and a 95 percent appearance rate at removal hearings (see Meissner and Kerwin, *DHS and Immigration*, p. 54).

60. U.S. Department of Homeland Security, Office of the Inspector General, "Detention and Removal of Illegal Aliens," OIG-06-33 (Washington, DC: Government Printing Office, April 2006), http://www.dhs.gov/xoig/assets/mgmtrpts/OIG_06-33_Apr06.pdf.

61. "Aggravated Felonies and Deportations," TRAC Immigration, June 9, 2006.

62. Suzanne Gamboa, "Citizens Held as Illegal Immigrants," Associated Press, April 13, 2009; Andrew Becker and Patrick J. McDonnell, "Immigration Sweeps Land Legal Resident in Detention with the Threat of Deportation," *Los Angeles Times*, April 9, 2009.

63. See the discussion in Henry G. Jarecki and Daniela Zane Kaisth, "Scholar Rescue in the Modern World," Institute of International Education, New York, 2009.

64. Warren Zimmerman, "Migrants and Refugees: A Threat to Security?" in Michael S. Teitelbaum and Myron Weiner, eds., *Threatened People, Threatened Borders: World Migration and U.S. Policy* (New York: W.W. Norton, 1995), p. 95.

65. There is much disagreement over the number of asylum claimants released into the United States who fail to show for their hearings and become absconders. Estimates from 2005, prior to the increase in the percentage of asylum seekers who are detained until their hearings, range from a low of about 6 percent to about 22 percent. See Bill Frelick, "U.S. Detention of Asylum Seekers and Human Rights," Migration Policy Institute, March 1, 2005, http://www.migrationinformation.org/USfocus/display.cfm?ID=296.

66. Human Rights First, "How to Repair the U.S. Asylum System: Blueprint for the Next Administration," December 2008.

67. Ibid.

68. Margaret Talbot, "The Lost Children: What do tougher detention policies mean for illegal immigrant families?" *New Yorker*, March 3, 2008.

69. See Donald Kerwin, "Revisiting the Need for Appointed Counsel," Migration Policy Institute, April 2005. See also the United States Committee on International Religious Freedom, "Asylum Seekers in Expedited Removal," February 8, 2005, which found that asylum seekers without a lawyer had only a 2 percent chance of their claims being granted, versus a 25 percent success rate for those with counsel.

70. "Report of the Special Rapporteur on the Human Rights of Migrants," Mission to the United States of America, United Nations General Assembly Human Rights Council, March 5, 2008.

71. "Asylum Seekers in Expedited Removal," United States Committee on International Religious Freedom, February 8, 2005. The study found some troubling patterns, such as the much higher rate of success for asylum applicants who could afford to obtain

legal counsel or were lucky enough to find pro bono representation (25 percent) than for those who did not have lawyers (just 2 percent).

72. Michael S. Teitelbaum, *Latin Migration North: The Problem for U.S. Foreign Policy* (New York: Council on Foreign Relations, 1985).

73. Moises Naim, "The New Diaspora," *Foreign Policy*, July/August 2002.

74. AnnaLee Saxenian, "Silicon Valley's New Immigrant Entrepreneurs," Public Policy Institute of California, 1999.

75. Vivek Wadhwa et al., "Intellectual Property, the Immigration Backlog, and a Reverse Brain-Drain: America's New Immigrant Entrepreneurs, Part III" (working paper, Duke University, August 22, 2007).

76. James E. Rauch, "Business and Social Networks in International Trade," *Journal of Economic Literature* vol. 39, no. 4 (December 2001), pp. 1177–203.

77. Michael Clemens, "Don't Close the Golden Door: Making Immigration Policy Work for Development" (policy brief, Center for Global Development, 2008).

78. Charlene Barshefsky, James T. Hill, and Shannon K. O'Neil, "U.S.-Latin America Relations: A New Direction for a New Reality," Independent Task Force Report No. 60 (New York: Council on Foreign Relations, 2008).

79. Michael Clemens and Lant Pritchett, "Income Per Natural: Measuring Development as if People Mattered More than Places" (Center for Global Development Working Paper No. 142, March 2008).

80. Gordon H. Hanson and Craig McIntosh, "The Great Mexican Emigration" (NBER Working Paper no. 13675, December 2007).

81. Barshefsky, Hill, and O'Neil, "U.S.-Latin America Relations."

82. Hanson and McIntosh, "The Great Mexican Emigration," p. 4.

83. Fernando Sedano, "Economic Implications of Mexico's Sudden Demographic Transition," *Business Economics*, July 1, 2008.

84. Shannon K. O'Neil, "Not Enough Immigrants," *Los Angeles Times*, April 5, 2007.

85. Gordon H. Hanson and Antonio Spilimbergo, "Illegal Immigration, Border Enforcement and Relative Wages: Evidence from Apprehensions at the U.S.-Mexico Border" (NBER Working Paper No. W5592, May 1996).

86. Pete Engardio and Geri Smith, "Mexico: Business is Standing its Ground," *BusinessWeek*, April 20, 2009.

87. Gordon H. Hanson, "Illegal Migration from Mexico to the United States," *Journal of Economic Literature* vol. 44, no. 4 (December 2006), pp. 869–924.

88. Richard Marosi, "Border Arrests Drop to 1970s Levels," *Los Angeles Times*, March 8, 2009.

89. Hanson and Spilimbergo, "Illegal Immigration, Border Enforcement, and Relative Wages," *American Economic Review* vol. 89 (1999), pp. 1337–57.

90. Commission for the Study of International Migration and Cooperative Economic Development, "Unauthorized Migration: An Economic Development Response" (Washington, DC: Government Printing Office, 1990).

91. Wayne Cornelius et al., "Controlling Unauthorized Immigration from Mexico: The Failure of 'Prevention Through Deterrence' and the Need for Comprehensive Reform" (briefing, Immigration Policy Center, June 10, 2008).

92. Douglas S. Massey, Jorge Durand, and Nolan J. Malone, *Beyond Smoke and Mirrors: Mexican Immigration in an Era of Economic Integration* (New York: Russell Sage Foundation, 2003); Douglas S. Massey, "Backfire at the Border: Why Enforcement Without Legalization Cannot Stop Illegal Immigration," Trade Policy Analysis No. 29 (Washington, DC: Cato Institute, Center for Trade Policy Studies, 2005).

93. Jeffrey Davidow, *The U.S. and Mexico: The Bear and the Porcupine* (Princeton, NJ: Markus Weiner, 2004); Jorge Castaneda, *Ex-Mex: From Migrants to Immigrants* (New York: New Press, 2008).

94. "U.S. Immigration Policy: Restoring Credibility" (report, U.S. Commission on Immigration Reform, 1994).

95. Fact Sheet: DHS End-of-Year Accomplishments, December 18, 2008.

96. Edward Alden, "Chertoff Battered but Not Bowed by Year in Office," *Financial Times*, March 13, 2006.

97. Gordon Hanson, *The Economic Logic of Illegal Immigration*, Council Special Report No. 26 (New York: Council on Foreign Relations, 2007).

98. Jeffrey Passel and D'Vera Cohn, "Trends in Unauthorized Immigration: Undocumented Inflow Now Trails Legal Inflow" (report, Pew Hispanic Center, October 2, 2008).

99. Hanson, *The Economic Logic of Illegal Immigration*.

100. U.S. Department of Homeland Security, "Yearbook of Immigration Statistics: 2008," table 7, http://www.dhs.gov/ximgtn/statistics/publications/LPR08.shtm.

101. "American Made: The Impact of Immigrant Entrepreneurs and Professionals on U.S. Competitiveness," National Venture Capital Association, November 2006.

102. Robert Pear, "A Point System for Immigrants Incites Passions," *New York Times*, June 5, 2007; Molly Hennessy-Fiske and Jim Puzzanghera, "Immigration Plan Doesn't Add Up, Critics Say," *Los Angeles Times*, May 24, 2007.

103. Letter from Western Governors Association to congressional leaders, April 9, 2008, http://www.westgov.org/wga/testim/Visa-Letter4-9-08.pdf.

104. Editorial, "A Cheap Shot at Workers," *New York Times*, December 15, 2008; "Bush Rewrites the Rules," *Los Angeles Times*, December 16, 2008.

105. See, for example, Philip L. Martin and Michael S. Teitelbaum, "The Mirage of Mexican Guest Workers," *Foreign Affairs*, November/December 2001.

106. See the excellent discussion in Alexandra Starr, "Europe Deals With Immigration," Slate.com, October 13–17, 2008, http://www.slate.com/id/2201909/entry/2201918.

107. Citizenship and Immigration Service Ombudsman, Annual Report 2007, U.S. Department of Homeland Security, June 11, 2007, p. iii.

108. Ibid, p. 8.

109. MPI, *Immigration and America's Future*, p. 35.

110. See U.S. Department of Homeland Security, "Yearbook of Immigration Statistics: 2008."

111. Vivek Wadhwa et al., "Intellectual Property, the Immigration Backlog, and a Reverse Brain-Drain: America's New Immigrant Entrepreneurs Part III," SSRN, August 22, 2007.

112. "Temporary Skilled Worker Visa Holders: Alberta, Canada welcomes you and your family," http://www.albertacanada.com/immigration/campaigns/h1b.html.

113. Meissner and Kerwin, *DHS and Immigration*, pp. 74–75.

114. Meissner and Kerwin, *DHS and Immigration*, pp. 71–74; DHS press release, "USCIS Revises Policy on Long-Pending FBI Name Checks," March 5, 2009.

115. See USCIS Fact Sheet, "USCIS Makes Major Strides During 2008," November 6, 2008; Meissner and Kerwin, *DHS and Immigration*, p. 72.

116. See Government Accountability Office, "Employment Verification: Challenges Exist in Implementing a Mandatory Electronic Employment Verification System," GAO-08-895T (Washington, DC: Government Printing Office, June 2008).

117. Meissner and Kerwin, *DHS and Immigration*, pp. 33–34.

118. Meissner and Kerwin, *DHS and Immigration*, p. 23.
119. Edward Alden, *The Closing of the American Border: Terrorism, Immigration and Security Since 9/11* (New York: HarperCollins, 2008).
120. See Kathleen Campbell Walker, "U.S. policy squeezes immigrants, not immigration," *National Law Journal*, May 25, 2009.
121. Deborah M. Weissman et al., The Policies and Politics of Local Immigration Enforcement Law" (report, American Civil Liberties Union and Immigration and Human Rights Policy Clinic, University of North Carolina, Chapel Hill, February 2009).
122. Passel and Cohn, "A Portrait of Unauthorized Immigrants."
123. Richard Land, "Immigration Reform and Southern Baptists" (press release, Ethics & Religious Liberty Commission, April 3, 2007), http://erlc.com/article/press-release-immigration-reform-and-southern-baptist/.
124. Christopher Sherman, "Passport Agency Questions Citizenship of Americans Delivered by Midwives near Mexico Border," *Associated Press*, February 10, 2009.
125. According to the Pew Hispanic Center, 5.4 percent of all jobs in the United States are held by undocumented workers, up from 4.3 percent in 2003. In Arizona, California and Nevada they comprise about 10 percent of the labor force (see Passel and Cohn, "A Portrait of Unauthorized Immigrants").
126. This recognition that undocumented workers can be used by unscrupulous employers to push down wages and working conditions was the basis for the historic April 2009 accord between the two larger labor union coalitions—the AFL-CIO and Change to Win—in support of comprehensive immigration reform ("The Labor Movement's Framework for Comprehensive Immigration Reform," April 2009, http://www.aflcio.org/issues/civilrights/immigration/upload/immigrationreform041409.pdf).
127. "Building an Americanization Movement for the Twenty-First Century: A Report to the President of the United States from the Task Force on New Americans," December 18, 2008.
128. Richard Akresh and Ilana Redstone Akresh, "Using Achievement Tests to Measure Language Assimilation and Language Bias Among Immigrant Children" (IZA Discussion Paper No. 3532, 2008); Ilana Redstone Akresh, "Contexts of English Language Use Among Immigrants to the United States," International Migration Review vol. 41, no. 4 (2007), pp. 930–55.
129. Kierkegaard, *The Accelerating Decline in America's High-Skilled Workforce*, pp. 79–80.
130. George Borjas, "An Evaluation of the Foreign Student Program," Center for Immigration Studies, June 2002.
131. Kirkegaard, *The Accelerating Decline in America's High-Skilled Workforce*, p. 82.
132. Meissner and Kerwin, *DHS and Immigration Policy*, p. 68.
133. MPI, *Immigration and America's Future*, p. 42.
134. A similar recommendation is contained in a recent report authored by Ray Marshall, who was secretary of labor in the Carter administration, which was endorsed by the labor union coalitions Change to Win and the AFL-CIO. He recommends the creation of a Foreign Worker Adjustment Commission, which is similar to the MPI proposal for a Standing Commission, though he would set "preservation of U.S. labor standards" as the commission's top priority and would set immigration levels based on whether companies have a demonstrable need for foreign labor. See Ray Marshall, *Immigration for Shared Prosperity: A Framework for Comprehensive Reform* (Washington, DC: Economic Policy Institute, 2009). The National Foundation for American Policy has strongly opposed the union recommendations, saying that the threshold of a certified labor shortage is far too high and would exclude most skilled immigration. It cautions that the MPI proposal could also be a "dangerous 'roll of the dice' for employers,

immigrants and their families." See "A Commission to Regulate Immigration? A Bad Idea Whose Time Should not Come" (policy brief, National Foundation for American Policy, May 2009).

135. This recommendation draws directly from the more detailed discussion in Meissner and Kerwin, *DHS and Immigration*, pp. 76–78.

136. National Research Council, *Beyond Fortress America*, pp. 47, 59.

137. Scales, "The Past and Present as Prologue."

138. "Secure Borders and Open Doors: Preserving Our Welcome to the World in an Age of Terrorism."

139. Thomas R. Eldridge et al., *9/11 and Terrorist Travel: A Staff Report of the National Commission on Terrorist Attacks Upon the United States* (Franklin, TN: Hillsboro Press, 2004).

140. U.S. Commission on International Religious Freedom, "Report on Asylum Seekers in Expedited Removal," and the follow-up report card issued in February 2007.

141. Some of these recommendations are taken from the excellent recent report, "The United States and Mexico: Towards a Strategic Partnership" (Washington, DC: Woodrow Wilson Center, Mexico Institute, January 2009).

Task Force Members

Task Force members are asked to join a consensus signifying that they endorse "the general policy thrust and judgments reached by the group, though not necessarily every finding and recommendation." They participate in the Task Force in their individual, not their institutional, capacities.

Edward Alden is the Bernard L. Schwartz senior fellow at the Council on Foreign Relations, where his research focuses on issues of U.S. economic competitiveness, including trade and immigration policy. Prior to joining CFR in 2007, he was the Washington bureau chief for the *Financial Times*. He also served as the *FT*'s bureau chief in Canada from 1998 to 2000. Previously, he was a senior reporter at the *Vancouver Sun* specializing in labor and employment issues as well as the managing editor of *Inside U.S. Trade*. He has won several national and international awards for his reporting, and writes for a wide variety of publications, including the *Washington Post*, *San Francisco Chronicle*, and *Toronto Globe & Mail*. His book, *The Closing of the American Border: Terrorism, Immigration and Security Since 9/11*, was named a "distinguished finalist" for the 2009 J. Anthony Lukas Book Prize for nonfiction. Alden holds a BA from the University of British Columbia and an MA in political science from the University of California, Berkeley.

Mary Boies founded the law firm Boies & McInnis LLP, which specializes in antitrust, securities, and corporate litigation. She chairs the executive committee of the Board of Business Executives for National Security. She is a member of the Dean's Executive Council at the Harvard Kennedy School of Government and on the Advisory Committee of MIT's Center for International Studies. She was appointed by the U.S. secretary of defense to the Air University Board of Visitors, whose purview includes the Air Force School for Advanced Air and Space

Studies, Air Command and Staff College, the College of Aerospace Doctrine, and the Air Force Institute of Technology. She serves on the Standing Committee on the Federal Judiciary, established by President Eisenhower to conduct professional peer reviews of nominees to the federal judiciary, including to the U.S. Supreme Court. She is founder and CEO of Mary Boies Software Inc., publisher of educational software. Previously, she was vice president and member of the law department at CBS Inc., general counsel of the U.S. Civil Aeronautics Board, assistant director of the White House Domestic Policy Staff, and counsel to the U.S. Senate Committee on Commerce.

Robert C. Bonner is a senior principal of the Sentinel HS Group and of counsel to Gibson, Dunn & Crutcher LLP. From 2003 through December 2005, Bonner served as the first commissioner of U.S. Customs and Border Protection, the agency of the Department of Homeland Security responsible for managing, controlling, and securing U.S. borders while facilitating global trade and travel. Bonner was appointed by President George W. Bush to serve as commissioner of U.S. Customs Service in September 2001. Before that, his government service included serving as administrator of the Drug Enforcement Administration from 1990 to 1993, as U.S. district judge for the Central District of California from 1989 to 1990, and as the U.S. attorney for the Central District of California from 1984 through 1989. Bonner is a fellow of the American College of Trial Lawyers. Bonner is also co-chair of the Pacific Council on International Policy's task force on U.S.-Mexico border policy, the Board of Trustees of the California Institute of Technology (Caltech), and the Board of Directors of the Homeland Security Advisory Council, Region One.

Jeb Bush is the president of Jeb Bush and Associates, LLC, a consulting firm. He served as the forty-third governor of Florida from 1999 to 2007. Before his election as governor, Bush worked as a real estate executive and pursued other entrepreneurial ventures in Florida from 1981 to 1998, and served as secretary of commerce for the state of Florida from 1987 to 1988. Before 1981, Bush served in various positions at Texas Commerce Bank in Houston, Texas, and in Caracas, Venezuela. He formed and serves as chairman of the Foundation for Florida's Future, a not-for-profit public policy organization, and the Foundation for Excellence in Education, a not-for-profit charitable organization.

Bush earned a BA in Latin American affairs from the University of Texas at Austin.

Allan E. Goodman is the sixth president of the Institute of International Education, the leading not-for-profit organization in the field of international educational exchange and development training. Previously, he was executive dean of the School of Foreign Service and professor at Georgetown University. He also served as presidential briefing coordinator for the director of Central Intelligence in the Carter administration. He has a BS from Northwestern University, an MPA from the Harvard Kennedy School, and a PhD in government from Harvard. Goodman also holds honorary doctorates from Toyota and Chatham universities, Middlebury, Mount Ida, and Ramapo colleges, and the State University of New York for his work in educational exchange and rescuing scholars. He has also received awards from Georgetown, Johns Hopkins, and Tufts universities, and the French Legion d'honneur.

Gordon H. Hanson is a professor of economics in the graduate school of international relations and Pacific studies and the department of economics at the University of California, San Diego (UCSD). He is also a research associate at the National Bureau of Economic Research and coeditor of the *Journal of Development Economics*. Before joining UCSD, he served on the faculties of the University of Michigan and the University of Texas. He is the author of more than fifty academic research publications on the economic consequences of immigration, international trade and investment, and other aspects of globalization. He is author of *Why Does Immigration Divide America? Public Finance and Political Opposition to Open Borders* and *Immigration Policy and the Welfare System.*

Michael H. Jordan is the former chairman and CEO of Electronic Data Systems (EDS). Prior to joining EDS, he was the retired chairman and chief executive officer of CBS Corporation (formerly Westinghouse Electric Corporation); partner with Clayton, Dubilier, and Rice; chairman and CEO of PepsiCo International; and a consultant and principal with McKinsey & Company. Jordan is a trustee of the Brookings Institution; a former member and chairman of the President's Export Council, a former chairman of the National Foreign Trade Council; a former chairman of the U.S.-Japan Business Council; a director and former chairman of the United Negro College Fund; a former chairman of the National Policy Board of the Americans for the Arts; and a former member of the following organizations: the Business Council, board of trustees of the United States Council for International Business, the international advisory board of British American Business Inc., and the Business Roundtable. He serves on the boards of several small, privately held companies and is a member of the Yale School of Management board of advisers. Jordan served a four-year tour of duty with the U.S. Navy on the staff of Admiral Hyman Rickover. He received a BS in chemical engineering from Yale University and an MS in chemical engineering from Princeton University.

Donald Kerwin is vice president for programs at the Migration Policy Institute (MPI), overseeing all of MPI's national and international programs. Before joining MPI, Kerwin worked for more than sixteen years at the Catholic Legal Immigration Network Inc. (CLINIC), serving as executive director for nearly fifteen years. CLINIC is a public interest legal corporation that supports a national network of 173 charitable legal programs for immigrants in more than 270 locations. On his arrival at CLINIC in 1992, Kerwin directed its political asylum project for Haitians. He became CLINIC's executive director in December 1993 and during his tenure, CLINIC coordinated the nation's largest political asylum, detainee services, immigration appeals, and naturalization programs. Kerwin is an adviser to the American Bar Association's Commission on Immigration, on the board of directors of Jesuit Refugee Services-USA, and an associate fellow at the Woodstock Theological Center. Mr. Kerwin is a 1984 graduate of Georgetown University and a 1989 graduate of the University of Michigan Law School.

Richard D. Land is president of the Ethics & Religious Liberty Commission, the Southern Baptist Convention's official entity assigned to address social, moral, and ethical concerns, with particular attention to their impact on American families and their faith. He has served in this position since October 1988. Before that, Land served as Criswell College's vice president for academic affairs from 1980 to 1988 and had taught as a professor of theology and church history at that institution since 1975. While on leave of absence from Criswell College, Land served from January 1987 to May 1988 as administrative assistant to the Honorable William P. Clements Jr., governor of Texas, as his senior adviser on church-state issues and areas relating to traditional family values. In 2005, *Time* magazine named Dr. Land as one of the "25 Most Influential Evangelicals." In October 2007, Senate Minority Leader Mitch McConnell of Kentucky appointed Land to a two-year term on the U.S. Commission on International Religious Freedom (USCIRF), an independent and bipartisan federal agency. This was Land's fourth appointment to USCIRF. In July 2005, then Senate Majority Leader Bill Frist had appointed Land, and President Bush selected Land for his first two terms (September 2001 to September 2004). He graduated with a BA (magna cum laude) from Princeton University and with a PhD from Oxford University in England. He also received an MT (Honors Program) degree from New Orleans Baptist Theological Seminary, where he served as student body president and received the Broadman Seminarian Award as the outstanding graduating student.

Elisa Massimino is CEO and executive director of Human Rights First, one of the nation's leading human rights advocacy organizations. Established in 1978, Human Rights First works in the United States and abroad to promote respect for human rights and the rule of law. Massimino joined Human Rights First in 1991 and served as the organization's Washington director for more than a decade before being named chief executive in September 2008. Massimino has a distinguished record of human rights advocacy in Washington. As a national authority on human rights law and policy, she has testified before Congress dozens of times and writes frequently for mainstream publications and specialized journals. In May 2008, the influential Washington newspaper *The Hill* named her one of the top twenty public advocates in the country. Massimino is a Phi Beta Kappa graduate of Trinity University in San Antonio, Texas, holds an MA in philosophy from Johns Hopkins University, and earned a law degree from the University of Michigan. Massimino serves as an adjunct professor at Georgetown University Law Center, where she teaches human rights advocacy. She is a member of the bar of the U.S. Supreme Court.

Thomas F. McLarty III has a distinguished record of business leadership and public service, including various roles advising U.S. presidents of both parties. He served as President Bill Clinton's first White House chief of staff, with more than five years in the president's cabinet and on the National Economic Council. He also organized the successful 1994

Summit of the Americas in Miami, which ultimately led to his appointment as special envoy for the Americas in 1997. After leaving the White House, McLarty returned to the private sector, where he had previously spent a decade as CEO of Arkla, a Fortune 500 natural gas company. He is currently president of McLarty Associates, an international strategic advisory firm, and also serves as chairman of the McLarty Companies, a fourth-generation family automotive business. McLarty remains an active participant in and commentator on hemispheric affairs. In 2001, he co-chaired the U.S.-Mexico Binational Migration Panel with Ambassador Andres Rozental. He is on the board of the Council of the Americas and the Inter-American Dialogue, as well as a number of private sector and philanthropic organizations. In addition, he serves as a senior international fellow at the U.S. Chamber of Commerce. McLarty graduated summa cum laude from the University of Arkansas.

Eliseo Medina has served as international executive vice president of the Service Employees International Union (SEIU) since 1996, when he made history by becoming the first Mexican-American elected to a top post at the two million-member SEIU. Medina's career as a labor activist began in 1965 when, as a nineteen-year-old grape-picker, he participated in the historic United Farm Workers' strike in Delano, California. Over the next thirteen years, Medina worked alongside labor leader and civil rights activist César Chávez and honed his skills as a union organizer and political strategist; eventually rising through the ranks to serve as the United Farm Workers' national vice president. Medina's interests in strategic organizing brought him to SEIU in 1986, where he helped revive a local union in San Diego—building its membership from 1,700 to over 10,000 in five years. He was one of the main strategists in the Los Angeles strike by SEIU Local 1877's building service workers, who in April 2000 won the largest wage increase in the fifteen-year history of SEIU's Justice for Janitors campaign. Medina also has a deeply felt interest in SEIU's work on immigration policies. In Los Angeles, he has helped strengthen ties between the Roman Catholic Church and the labor movement to work on common concerns such as immigrant worker rights and access to health care.

Steve Padilla is a public policy and land use consultant currently serving as president and chief executive officer of the Aquarius Group Inc. He served as mayor of the city of Chula Vista, California, from 2002 to 2006 and as a member of the California Coastal Commission from 2005 to 2007. He also served two terms on Chula Vista's City Council from 1994 to 2002 before being elected mayor. Padilla served in numerous San Diego County local and regional offices and held statewide and national affiliations during his term as mayor, including the board of the San Diego Association of Governments, the League of California Cities, and the United States Conference of Mayors. Before his elected career, Padilla was a detective with the Coronado Police Department and a high school teacher. He remains active in local, state, and national public affairs, and currently writes a monthly public affairs column for *La Prensa San Diego*. He earned a BPA from National University.

Robert D. Putnam is the Peter and Isabel Malkin professor of public policy at Harvard University, where he teaches both undergraduate and graduate courses. He is also visiting professor and director of the Manchester Graduate Summer Programme in Social Change, University of Manchester (UK). Putnam is a member of the National Academy of Sciences, a fellow of the British Academy, and past president of the American Political Science Association. In 2006, Putnam received the Skytte Prize, one of the world's highest accolades for a political scientist. He has served as dean of the Harvard Kennedy School. He has written a dozen books, translated into seventeen languages, including two, *Making Democracy Work* and *Bowling Alone*, which rank high among the most cited publications in the social sciences worldwide in the last several decades. He founded the Saguaro Seminar, bringing together leading thinkers and practitioners to develop actionable ideas for civic renewal. Before coming to Harvard in 1979, he taught at the University of Michigan and served on the staff of the National Security Council. Putnam graduated from Swarthmore College in 1963, won a Fulbright Fellowship to study at Balliol College, Oxford, and went on to earn master's and doctorate degrees from Yale University, the latter in 1970.

Andrew D. Selee is director of the Woodrow Wilson Center's Mexico Institute, which promotes dialogue and policy research on U.S.-Mexico relations. He served previously as senior program associate of the Latin American program and as professional staff in the U.S. House of Representatives and worked for five years in Mexico. He is editor or coeditor of several publications on U.S.-Mexico relations, Mexican politics, immigration, and decentralization. Selee is an adjunct professor of government at Johns Hopkins University and has been a visiting scholar at El Colegio de México. He is a board member of the U.S.-Mexico Fulbright Commission (Comexus) and a contributing editor to the *Handbook of Latin American Studies*. A long-time volunteer of the YMCA, Selee served for five years on the National Board of the YMCA of the USA and chaired its International Committee.

Margaret D. Stock is an attorney admitted in Alaska and a lieutenant colonel, Military Police Corps, U.S. Army Reserve. From 1993 to 2001, she practiced law in Alaska, where she was an associate at a general trial practice firm and then the managing partner at a firm that emphasized immigration and citizenship law. From June 2001 to June 2006, she was a Title 10 civilian professor in the department of law at the United States Military Academy, West Point, New York, after which she accepted an assignment as a drilling individual mobilization augmentee (DIMA) (associate professor) in West Point's Department of Social Sciences. In 2005, the American Immigration Lawyers Association awarded her its prestigious Advocacy Award for her work informing Congress and the public about the connection between immigration and national security. She is also a 2006 graduate of the Army War College, which awarded her a master of strategic studies degree. Stock was instrumental in the creation of AILA's Military Assistance Program, and is a member of the editorial board of *Bender's Immigration Bulletin*. She earned an AB in government at Harvard-Radcliffe in 1985, a JD at Harvard Law School in 1992, and an MPA at the Harvard Kennedy School in 2001.

Frances Fragos Townsend is currently a corporate partner at Baker Botts, LLP. Previously she served as assistant to President George W. Bush for homeland security and counterterrorism and chaired the Homeland Security Council from May 2004 until January 2008, and as deputy assistant to the president and deputy national security adviser for combating terrorism from May 2003 to May 2004. Before serving the president, Townsend was the first assistant commandant for intelligence for the U. S. Coast Guard. She began her prosecutorial career in 1985 as an assistant district attorney in Brooklyn, New York, and then joined the U.S. Attorney's Office for the Southern District of New York. In 1991, she worked in the Office of the Attorney General to assist in establishing the newly created Office of International Programs, and in

1993 joined the Criminal Division as chief of staff to the assistant attorney general. Townsend was director of the Office of International Affairs in the Criminal Division from November 1995 to November 1997, after which she was appointed acting deputy assistant attorney general for the Criminal Division. In March 1998, Townsend was appointed counsel for intelligence policy, in which capacity she headed the Department of Justice's Office of Intelligence Policy and Review. She has a BA in political science and a BS in psychology from American University, and a JD from the University of San Diego School of Law. In 1986, she attended the Institute on International and Comparative Law in London.

Kathleen Campbell Walker is the immediate past national president of the American Immigration Lawyers Association, and is board certified in immigration and nationality law by the Texas Board of Legal Specialization. She currently heads the immigration and international trade group of Brown McCarroll, LLP, headquartered in Austin. Walker's immigration law practice primarily focuses on business and family-based immigration, consular processing, employer sanctions, citizenship and naturalization, security checks, and admission issues. She has frequently provided testimony before Congress as well as the Texas House and Senate, and has practiced on the border in El Paso for over twenty-three years. She served as the chairperson of the Exam Committee on Immigration and Nationality Law for several years for the Texas Board of Legal Specialization and was named in 2008 as one of the thirty women recognized in the "Extraordinary Women in Texas Law" publication of the *Texas Lawyer*. Walker earned a BA from Texas Tech University and a JD from the University of Texas School of Law.

Raul H. Yzaguirre is currently presidential professor of practice in community development and civil rights at Arizona State University, where he is helping to establish a center focused on community development, education for practitioners, and academic scholarship. He served as president and chief executive officer of the National Council of La Raza, the largest national Hispanic constituency-based organization in the United States and the leading Hispanic think tank in Washington, DC, from 1974 to 2004. He was the first Hispanic to serve on the executive committee of the Leadership Conference on Civil Rights, was chairperson of President Clinton's Advisory Commission on Educational Excellence for Hispanic Americans, and was a fellow at the Institute of Politics at the Harvard Kennedy School. After serving four years in the U.S. Air Force Medical Corps, Yzaguirre founded the National Organization for Mexican American Services. After this, he worked as a senior program officer at the migrant division of the U.S. Office of Economic Opportunity before founding Interstate Research Associates, the first Latino research association, which he built into a multimillion-dollar nonprofit consulting firm. Yzaguirre received his BS from George Washington University.

Task Force Observers

Observers participate in Task Force discussions, but are not asked to join the consensus. They participate in their individual, not institutional, capacities.

Max Boot is the Jeane J. Kirkpatrick senior fellow in National Security studies at the Council on Foreign Relations in New York. He is also a contributing editor to the *Weekly Standard* and *Los Angeles Times*, and a regular contributor to the *New York Times*, *Wall Street Journal*, *Foreign Affairs*, *Commentary*, and many other publications. His last book, *War Made New: Technology, Warfare, and the Course of History, 1500 to Today*, has been hailed as a "magisterial survey of technology and war" by the *New York Times*, "brilliantly crafted history" by the *Wall Street Journal*, and "a book for both the general reader and reading generals" by the *New York Post*. His previous book, *The Savage Wars of Peace: Small Wars and the Rise of American Power*, was selected as one of the best books of 2002 by the *Washington Post*, the *Los Angeles Times*, and the *Christian Science Monitor*. He is a member of the U.S. Joint Forces Command Transformation Advisory Group and was a senior foreign policy adviser to John McCain's presidential campaign in 2007–2008. Before joining CFR in 2002, Boot spent eight years as a writer and editor at the *Wall Street Journal*, the last five years as editorial features editor. From 1992 to 1994 he was an editor and writer at the *Christian Science Monitor*. Boot holds a BA in history, with high honors, from the University of California, Berkeley and an MA in history from Yale University.

Andrew Kohut is the president of the Pew Research Center. He also acts as director of the Pew Research Center for the People & the Press (formerly the Times Mirror Center for the People & the Press) and the Pew Global Attitudes Project. He was president of the Gallup Organization from 1979 to 1989. In 1989, he founded Princeton Survey

Research Associates, an attitude and opinion research firm specializing in media, politics, and public policy studies. He served as founding director of surveys for the Times Mirror Center from 1990 to 1992, and was named its director in 1993. He is a past president of the American Association of Public Opinion Research and the National Council on Public Polls. In 2005, he received the American Association of Public Opinion Research's highest honor, the Award for Exceptionally Distinguished Achievement. He is a frequent press commentator on the meaning and interpretation of opinion poll results and the coauthor of four books, including, mostly recently, *America Against the World*. He received an AB degree from Seton Hall University in 1964 and studied graduate sociology at Rutgers, the State University, from 1964 to 1966.

Shannon K. O'Neil is the Douglas Dillon fellow for Latin America studies at the Council on Foreign Relations. Her expertise includes political and economic reform in Latin America, U.S.-Latin America relations, and Latin American immigration to the United States. She recently directed CFR's Independent Task Force on U.S.-Latin America Relations. She is currently working on a book on Mexico, analyzing the political, economic, and social transformations Mexico has undergone over the last two decades, and the significance of these changes for U.S.-Mexico relations. In addition to her work at CFR, O'Neil has taught in the political science department at Columbia University, and she publishes LatIntelligence—www.latintelligence.com—a blog analyzing Latin American politics, economics, and public policies. Before joining CFR, she was a justice, welfare, and economics fellow, and an executive committee member and graduate associate at the Weatherhead Center for International Affairs at Harvard University. She was also a Fulbright Scholar in Mexico and Argentina. Before her academic work, O'Neil worked in the private sector as an equity analyst at Indosuez Capital Latin America and Credit Lyonnais Securities. She holds a BA from Yale University, an MA in international relations from Yale University, and a PhD in government from Harvard University.

Julia E. Sweig is the Nelson and David Rockefeller senior fellow for Latin America studies and director Latin America studies at the Council on Foreign Relations. She is the author of *Friendly Fire: Losing Friends and Making Enemies in the Anti-American Century*, as well as numerous scholarly articles, opinion pieces, and congressional testimonies on

Cuba, Colombia, Venezuela, Latin America, and American foreign policy. She has directed several Council on Foreign Relations reports on the Andean region and on Cuba, and served most recently as senior adviser for CFR's Independent Task Force on U.S.-Latin America Relations. Sweig's *Inside the Cuban Revolution: Fidel Castro and the Urban Underground* received the American Historical Association's Herbert Feis Award for best book of the year by an independent scholar. Her new book, *Cuba: What Everyone Needs to Know*, was released in June 2009.

Independent Task Force Reports

Published by the Council on Foreign Relations

U.S. Nuclear Weapons Policy
William J. Perry and Brent Scowcroft, Chairs; Charles D. Ferguson, Project Director
Independent Task Force Report No. 62 (2009)

Confronting Climate Change: A Strategy for U.S. Foreign Policy
George E. Pataki and Thomas J. Vilsack, Chairs; Michael A. Levi, Project Director
Independent Task Force Report No. 61 (2008)

U.S.-Latin America Relations: A New Direction for a New Reality
Charlene Barshefsky and James T. Hill, Chairs; Shannon O'Neil, Project Director
Independent Task Force Report No. 60 (2008)

U.S.-China Relations: An Affirmative Agenda, A Responsible Course
Carla A. Hills and Dennis C. Blair, Chairs; Frank Sampson Jannuzi, Project Director
Independent Task Force Report No. 59 (2007)

National Security Consequences of U.S. Oil Dependency
John Deutch and James R. Schlesinger, Chairs; David G. Victor, Project Director
Independent Task Force Report No. 58 (2006)

Russia's Wrong Direction: What the United States Can and Should Do
John Edwards and Jack Kemp, Chairs; Stephen Sestanovich, Project Director
Independent Task Force Report No. 57 (2006)

More than Humanitarianism: A Strategic U.S. Approach Toward Africa
Anthony Lake and Christine Todd Whitman, Chairs; Princeton N. Lyman and J. Stephen
Morrison, Project Directors
Independent Task Force Report No. 56 (2006)

In the Wake of War: Improving Post-Conflict Capabilities
Samuel R. Berger and Brent Scowcroft, Chairs; William L. Nash, Project Director; Mona K.
Sutphen, Deputy Director
Independent Task Force Report No. 55 (2005)

In Support of Arab Democracy: Why and How
Madeleine K. Albright and Vin Weber, Chairs; Steven A. Cook, Project Director
Independent Task Force Report No. 54 (2005)

Building a North American Community
John P. Manley, Pedro Aspe, and William F. Weld, Chairs; Thomas d'Aquino, Andrés
Rozental, and Robert Pastor, Vice Chairs; Chappell H. Lawson, Project Director
Independent Task Force Report No. 53 (2005)

Iran: Time for a New Approach
Zbigniew Brzezinski and Robert M. Gates, Chairs; Suzanne Maloney, Project Director
Independent Task Force Report No. 52 (2004)

An Update on the Global Campaign Against Terrorist Financing
Maurice R. Greenberg, Chair; William F. Wechsler and Lee S. Wolosky, Project Directors
Independent Task Force Report No. 40B (Web-only release, 2004)

Renewing the Atlantic Partnership
Henry A. Kissinger and Lawrence H. Summers, Chairs; Charles A. Kupchan, Project Director
Independent Task Force Report No. 51 (2004)

Iraq: One Year After
Thomas R. Pickering and James R. Schlesinger, Chairs; Eric P. Schwartz, Project Consultant
Independent Task Force Report No. 43C (Web-only release, 2004)

Nonlethal Weapons and Capabilities
Paul X. Kelley and Graham Allison, Chairs; Richard L. Garwin, Project Director
Independent Task Force Report No. 50 (2004)

*New Priorities in South Asia: U.S. Policy Toward India, Pakistan, and Afghanistan
(Chairmen's Report)*
Marshall Bouton, Nicholas Platt, and Frank G. Wisner, Chairs; Dennis Kux and Mahnaz
Ispahani, Project Directors
Independent Task Force Report No. 49 (2003)
Cosponsored with the Asia Society

Finding America's Voice: A Strategy for Reinvigorating U.S. Public Diplomacy
Peter G. Peterson, Chair; Kathy Bloomgarden, Henry Grunwald, David E. Morey, and
Shibley Telhami, Working Committee Chairs; Jennifer Sieg, Project Director; Sharon
Herbstman, Project Coordinator
Independent Task Force Report No. 48 (2003)

Emergency Responders: Drastically Underfunded, Dangerously Unprepared
Warren B. Rudman, Chair; Richard A. Clarke, Senior Adviser; Jamie F. Metzl, Project
Director
Independent Task Force Report No. 47 (2003)

Iraq: The Day After (Chairs' Update)
Thomas R. Pickering and James R. Schlesinger, Chairs; Eric P. Schwartz, Project Director
Independent Task Force Report No. 43B (Web-only release, 2003)

Burma: Time for Change
Mathea Falco, Chair
Independent Task Force Report No. 46 (2003)

Afghanistan: Are We Losing the Peace?
Marshall Bouton, Nicholas Platt, and Frank G. Wisner, Chairs; Dennis Kux and Mahnaz
Ispahani, Project Directors
Chairman's Report of an Independent Task Force (2003)
Cosponsored with the Asia Society

Meeting the North Korean Nuclear Challenge
Morton I. Abramowitz and James T. Laney, Chairs; Eric Heginbotham, Project Director
Independent Task Force Report No. 45 (2003)

Chinese Military Power
Harold Brown, Chair; Joseph W. Prueher, Vice Chair; Adam Segal, Project Director
Independent Task Force Report No. 44 (2003)

Iraq: The Day After
Thomas R. Pickering and James R. Schlesinger, Chairs; Eric P. Schwartz, Project Director
Independent Task Force Report No. 43 (2003)

Threats to Democracy: Prevention and Response
Madeleine K. Albright and Bronislaw Geremek, Chairs; Morton H. Halperin, Director;
Elizabeth Frawley Bagley, Associate Director
Independent Task Force Report No. 42 (2002)

America—Still Unprepared, Still in Danger
Gary Hart and Warren B. Rudman, Chairs; Stephen E. Flynn, Project Director
Independent Task Force Report No. 41 (2002)

Terrorist Financing
Maurice R. Greenberg, Chair; William F. Wechsler and Lee S. Wolosky, Project Directors
Independent Task Force Report No. 40 (2002)

Enhancing U.S. Leadership at the United Nations
David Dreier and Lee H. Hamilton, Chairs; Lee Feinstein and Adrian Karatnycky, Project
Directors
Independent Task Force Report No. 39 (2002)
Cosponsored with Freedom House

Improving the U.S. Public Diplomacy Campaign in the War Against Terrorism
Carla A. Hills and Richard C. Holbrooke, Chairs; Charles G. Boyd, Project Director
Independent Task Force Report No. 38 (Web-only release, 2001)

Building Support for More Open Trade
Kenneth M. Duberstein and Robert E. Rubin, Chairs; Timothy F. Geithner, Project
Director; Daniel R. Lucich, Deputy Project Director
Independent Task Force Report No. 37 (2001)

Beginning the Journey: China, the United States, and the WTO
Robert D. Hormats, Chair; Elizabeth Economy and Kevin Nealer, Project Directors
Independent Task Force Report No. 36 (2001)

Strategic Energy Policy Update
Edward L. Morse, Chair; Amy Myers Jaffe, Project Director
Independent Task Force Report No. 33B (2001)
Cosponsored with the James A. Baker III Institute for Public Policy of Rice University

Testing North Korea: The Next Stage in U.S. and ROK Policy
Morton I. Abramowitz and James T. Laney, Chairs; Robert A. Manning, Project Director
Independent Task Force Report No. 35 (2001)

The United States and Southeast Asia: A Policy Agenda for the New Administration
J. Robert Kerrey, Chair; Robert A. Manning, Project Director
Independent Task Force Report No. 34 (2001)

Strategic Energy Policy: Challenges for the 21st Century
Edward L. Morse, Chair; Amy Myers Jaffe, Project Director
Independent Task Force Report No. 33 (2001)
Cosponsored with the James A. Baker III Institute for Public Policy of Rice University

A Letter to the President and a Memorandum on U.S Policy Toward Brazil
Stephen Robert, Chair; Kenneth Maxwell, Project Director
Independent Task Force Report No. 32 (2001)

State Department Reform
Frank C. Carlucci, Chair; Ian J. Brzezinski, Project Coordinator
Independent Task Force Report No. 31 (2001)
Cosponsored with the Center for Strategic and International Studies

U.S.-Cuban Relations in the 21st Century: A Follow-on Report
Bernard W. Aronson and William D. Rogers, Chairs; Julia Sweig and Walter Mead, Project
Directors
Independent Task Force Report No. 30 (2000)

Toward Greater Peace and Security in Colombia: Forging a Constructive U.S. Policy
Bob Graham and Brent Scowcroft, Chairs; Michael Shifter, Project Director
Independent Task Force Report No. 29 (2000)
Cosponsored with the Inter-American Dialogue

Future Directions for U.S. Economic Policy Toward Japan
Laura D'Andrea Tyson, Chair; M. Diana Helweg Newton, Project Director
Independent Task Force Report No. 28 (2000)

First Steps Toward a Constructive U.S. Policy in Colombia
Bob Graham and Brent Scowcroft, Chairs; Michael Shifter, Project Director
Interim Report (2000)
Cosponsored with the Inter-American Dialogue

Promoting Sustainable Economies in the Balkans
Steven Rattner, Chair; Michael B.G. Froman, Project Director
Independent Task Force Report No. 27 (2000)

Non-Lethal Technologies: Progress and Prospects
Richard L. Garwin, Chair; W. Montague Winfield, Project Director
Independent Task Force Report No. 26 (1999)

Safeguarding Prosperity in a Global Financial System: The Future International Financial Architecture
Carla A. Hills and Peter G. Peterson, Chairs; Morris Goldstein, Project Director
Independent Task Force Report No. 25 (1999)
Cosponsored with the International Institute for Economics

U.S. Policy Toward North Korea: Next Steps
Morton I. Abramowitz and James T. Laney, Chairs; Michael J. Green, Project Director
Independent Task Force Report No. 24 (1999)

Reconstructing the Balkans
Morton I. Abramowitz and Albert Fishlow, Chairs; Charles A. Kupchan, Project Director
Independent Task Force Report No. 23 (Web-only release, 1999)

Strengthening Palestinian Public Institutions
Michel Rocard, Chair; Henry Siegman, Project Director; Yezid Sayigh and Khalil Shikaki, Principal Authors
Independent Task Force Report No. 22 (1999)

U.S. Policy Toward Northeastern Europe
Zbigniew Brzezinski, Chair; F. Stephen Larrabee, Project Director
Independent Task Force Report No. 21 (1999)

The Future of Transatlantic Relations
Robert D. Blackwill, Chair and Project Director
Independent Task Force Report No. 20 (1999)

U.S.-Cuban Relations in the 21st Century
Bernard W. Aronson and William D. Rogers, Chairs; Walter Russell Mead, Project Director
Independent Task Force Report No. 19 (1999)

After the Tests: U.S. Policy Toward India and Pakistan
Richard N. Haass and Morton H. Halperin, Chairs
Independent Task Force Report No. 18 (1998)
Cosponsored with the Brookings Institution

Managing Change on the Korean Peninsula
Morton I. Abramowitz and James T. Laney, Chairs; Michael J. Green, Project Director
Independent Task Force Report No. 17 (1998)

Promoting U.S. Economic Relations with Africa
Peggy Dulany and Frank Savage, Chairs; Salih Booker, Project Director
Independent Task Force Report No. 16 (1998)

U.S. Middle East Policy and the Peace Process
Henry Siegman, Project Coordinator
Independent Task Force Report No. 15 (1997)

Differentiated Containment: U.S. Policy Toward Iran and Iraq
Zbigniew Brzezinski and Brent Scowcroft, Chairs; Richard W. Murphy, Project Director
Independent Task Force Report No. 14 (1997)

Russia, Its Neighbors, and an Enlarging NATO
Richard G. Lugar, Chair; Victoria Nuland, Project Director
Independent Task Force Report No. 13 (1997)

Rethinking International Drug Control: New Directions for U.S. Policy
Mathea Falco, Chair
Independent Task Force Report No. 12 (1997)

Financing America's Leadership: Protecting American Interests and Promoting American Values
Mickey Edwards and Stephen J. Solarz, Chairs; Morton H. Halperin, Lawrence J. Korb, and
Richard M. Moose, Project Directors
Independent Task Force Report No. 11 (1997)
Cosponsored with the Brookings Institution

A New U.S. Policy Toward India and Pakistan
Richard N. Haass, Chair; Gideon Rose, Project Director
Independent Task Force Report No. 10 (1997)

Arms Control and the U.S.-Russian Relationship
Robert D. Blackwill, Chair and Author; Keith W. Dayton, Project Director
Independent Task Force Report No. 9 (1996)
Cosponsored with the Nixon Center for Peace and Freedom

American National Interest and the United Nations
George Soros, Chair
Independent Task Force Report No. 8 (1996)

Making Intelligence Smarter: The Future of U.S. Intelligence
Maurice R. Greenberg, Chair; Richard N. Haass, Project Director
Independent Task Force Report No. 7 (1996)

Lessons of the Mexican Peso Crisis
John C. Whitehead, Chair; Marie-Josée Kravis, Project Director
Independent Task Force Report No. 6 (1996)

Managing the Taiwan Issue: Key Is Better U.S. Relations with China
Stephen Friedman, Chair; Elizabeth Economy, Project Director
Independent Task Force Report No. 5 (1995)

Non-Lethal Technologies: Military Options and Implications
Malcolm H. Wiener, Chair
Independent Task Force Report No. 4 (1995)

Should NATO Expand?
Harold Brown, Chair; Charles A. Kupchan, Project Director
Independent Task Force Report No. 3 (1995)

Success or Sellout? The U.S.-North Korean Nuclear Accord
Kyung Won Kim and Nicholas Platt, Chairs; Richard N. Haass, Project Director
Independent Task Force Report No. 2 (1995)
Cosponsored with the Seoul Forum for International Affairs

Nuclear Proliferation: Confronting the New Challenges
Stephen J. Hadley, Chair; Mitchell B. Reiss, Project Director
Independent Task Force Report No. 1 (1995)

To purchase a printed copy, call the Brookings Institution Press: 800.537.5487.
Note: Task Force reports are available for download from CFR's website, www.cfr.org.
For more information, email publications@cfr.org.